Islamic State:
The Countdown Has Begun

D.J. Ratkowski

Edited by Julian Sander

Special Thanks
To
John Biery & Donald Huxtable

Cover design by D.J.Ratkowski
Copyright © 2015 D.J. Ratkowski

ISBN: 1508482462
ISBN-13: 978-1508482468

DEDICATION

I dedicate this book to my wife and children for being the inspiration in my life and having the patience to let me be me.

CONTENTS

FORWARD

The information contained herein chronicles the rise of the Islamic State and Islamic extremism around the globe. This book is the result of a desire to understand a new kind of enemy rising from the sands of the Middle East. The Western world is facing an old adversary in a new era and the west must once again prepare for the approaching clash of ideals. My search for understanding began during the first Gulf War. As a United States Marine in the hot desert sands of Iraq, I embarked on a journey to clearly understand my enemy. I had plenty of questions and was looking for some answers. What makes this the Holy Land which so many have fought and died for? Why did Iraq invade Kuwait? Does Iraq possess weapons of mass destruction? What really is in Afghanistan? What are we really doing in the Middle East?

I began researching the many questions I had and what started out as a subtle desire to raise my level of awareness, soon became an unquenchable thirst for knowledge. This quest for information took me farther into the past than I had anticipated. In order to understand todays volatile sands of the Middle East I had to trace the roots of al-Qaeda back almost forty years. Back to a time when they recruited covertly within the United States while using U.S. Government grants to fund the process.

It is apparent much of the Middle East has been used as a political playground by the worlds governing administrations for the past century. As a result of the political vacuums created by unstable governments within the region, the Middle East is being snatched up by modern day marauders in the name of Islam. Meanwhile the search continues for ways to combat the growing affliction of Muslim hatred threatening to consume the Western World. The threat of the Islamic State in America is real and it is significant. This is a war that will be fought in a myriad of ways and this book was written to help prepare for the dark days ahead. Make sure you are ready.

JIHAD

Since the beginning of Islam the sounds of jihad have been carried across the desert sands. The West's first encounter with jihad was in 1095 when Pope Urban II proclaimed the first Crusade to restore access to Jerusalem and the Holy Land. The word "Jihad" translated means "struggling" or "striving." It is often mistranslated and interpreted as Holy War. In a religious sense when addressing the Holy Qur'an or the teachings of the Prophet Muhammad the word "Jihad" can take on many meanings. This ambiguity has allowed the concept of jihad to be used by political and religious groups throughout history to justify violence. In many cases the Holy Qur'an refers to the jihad of the soul, the struggle to walk the path of God. This inner strife would be considered the "Greater Jihad," and the act of war or outer struggle would be regarded as the "Lessor Jihad."

The term Holy War was used by the crusaders to justify the invasion of the Holy Land. A two hundred year struggle to control the Holy cities and their surrounding lands would follow, encompassing six more major crusades. Each would ultimately end the way they began with Islam again in control of the majority of the region.

The desert is an extreme and unforgiving environment that tests the souls of those who inhabit it. I know this from my time spent under the blazing sun in the Middle East. Time spent in the harsh conditions also taught me that Muslims have a long history of fighting amongst themselves. It is important to have a basic understanding of the rift between Sunni and Shi'ite Muslims, a divide dating back to the death of the Prophet Muhammed. Sunni are the majority and account for about 80% of Muslims throughout the world. Shi'ite and Sunni Muslims have been struggling with their differences for over a thousand years, and what we are witnessing now is the 21st century evolution of their ideological difference.

The continuous infighting between Sunni and Shi'ite is one of the reasons the Middle East has been so susceptible to outside influence. It is also one of the reasons the early crusades into the Holy Land were so successful. However, there have been rare moments in history where strong men, rich with ideals, have united Muslims to a single cause. One such man who inspired many was named Saladin.

Saladin was a Sunni Muslim born to a military Kurdish family in the 12th century. He was a natural leader and rose quickly under the tutelage of a Syrian Mesopotamian military leader, Nur al-Din. Under the Shi'ite Fatimid Dynasty, Saladin participated in three large military campaigns into Egypt.[1] In 1169 Saladin would become the leader of the expeditionary military forces and advisor to the Shi'ite Caliph (leader) in Cairo. He used that position to undermine and eliminate Fatimid's infantry slave forces and in 1171 brought an end to the Shi'ite Fatimid Caliphate in honor of the Sunni Caliphate in Baghdad.[2] Saladin, a wise military leader, recognized that he must first fight Muslims before he would be able to battle invading Westerners. He understood that a divided Muslim nation would be no match for the crusading Christian Knights on a mission from God. By eliminating the Shi'ite caliph, Saladin created a single powerful state to unite Muslims in his cause to vanquish the crusaders and reclaim the Holy Lands. He knew that he must also unite the Muslims through the religious teachings of Islam, in much the same way the Christians were united in their cause. In October of 1187 Saladin's forces defeated the crusaders and reclaimed Jerusalem.[3]

Today the word jihad is once more being used to sound the drums of war. The desert is again filled with turmoil as a new Islamic State has begun a cleansing of the great sands. Christians and Shi'ite Muslims, along with those deemed apostates are being slain in an effort to reclaim the Holy Land. The Islamic State is not only driving out the infidels, but also those who do not recognize and adopt the strict adherence of sharia law. Enormous efforts are being made to reclaim lost power throughout the region as we see the one finger gesture proudly proclaiming a unified Islamic State.

I draw the parallels to Saladin because once again a strong leader has risen to unite the Sunni Muslims to a singular purpose using the teachings of Islam with an understanding that he must first fight Muslims before he can fight the infidels. It is the black and white flag of the Islamic State that can be seen leading the way as extreme Sunni Muslims flock to the banner of what they believe will be the final jihad.

One key to understanding jihad and it's many meanings, is to first look to who is using the word, that will tell you which of the various definitions is being interpreted. To interpret how the term jihad is being used by the Islamic State we need only to examine recent history and view the role of al-Qaeda in the Middle East.

In order to pinpoint the origin of al-Qaeda first let us

examine the Soviet conflict in Afghanistan during the late 1970s and 1980s. During this period of aggressive soviet expansionism we can see the Soviet backed Marxist government in conflict with the freedom fighters, or Mujahideen, Afghan natives. A person engaged in jihad is called Mujahid, and the plural form or reference too many engaged in jihad is Mujahideen. A large percentage of the freedom fighters or Mujahideen were in fact Islamic militants. An operation called "Cyclone" was initiated by the CIA to direct funds through Pakistan's Inter-Services Intelligence Agency. This was how the U.S. Government discreetly funded the Islamic militants engaging Soviet troops during the Cold War era.[4]

One organization of note would be the Maktab al-Khidamat (MAK). This particular organization was lobbied for by Osama Bin Laden and funded by the Saudi government, business professionals, and organizations sympathetic to Muslim plights. MAK had the ability to generate over half a billion dollars annually to fund the jihad in Afghanistan. With a seemingly endless influx of money and support, MAK continued to grow and soon established training facilities in Peshawar and Afghanistan.

In 1986, with the help of Ali Mohamed and Omar Abdel-Rahman, the first recruitment center was established in the United States. The Al Kifah Refugee Center was set up and managed by MAK in Brooklyn, New York, while receiving U.S. Government funding for Afghan relief aid. Many believe this is where al-Qaeda was born.[5]

By 1987 Omar Abdel-Rahman, also known as the "Blind Sheikh," a well-known recruiter of Mujahideen for Afghanistan, had established a network of recruiting stations within the United States. Meanwhile Osama Bin Laden had constructed multiple training camps inside Afghanistan and Pakistan. It is estimated that MAK is responsible for recruiting over 35,000 Mujahideen fighters, from 43 different foreign countries, to participate in the

Soviet-Afghan war over a ten year period.[6] The U.S. financial support to the Afghan militants, or Islamic fighters, was significant and played a major role in developing the resources, tactics and networks needed to allow MAK to continue to thrive.

In August of 1988 it was the combination of Ali-Mohamed, Osama Bin Laden, and Omar Abdel-Rahman that masterminded the creation of al-Qaeda.[7] The name and organization was kept a secret as they continued to raise funds for the Mujahideen fighters, and eventually in 1989 over 250,000 Islamic militants drove the Soviet Union form Afghanistan. However, once the Soviet forces withdrew from Afghanistan the government was considerably weakened and eventually overrun by the Mujahideen fighters.

Due to constant infighting the victory of the Mujahideen was fleeting, as the conquering tribal leaders of Afghanistan were unable to establish a functioning government. For a brief period of time there was a continual restructuring of alliances as the fight for control of different territories ensued. As a result disorder soon followed and the country fell into disarray. It was at this time that some Mujahideen wanted to expand their fight and take up other causes on a global scale. Bin Laden however returned to Saudi Arabia in February of 1989 to begin establishing non-military operations around the world.[8] Abdullah Azzam is considered by many to be the father of global jihad.[9] He was also a leader in the MAK organization and was not pleased when Osama began working on non-military operations, Abdullah Azzam instead wanted to maintain the funding of the training camps and continue focusing on military campaigns. Abdullah Azzam was assassinated by use of a car bomb in November of 1989 and shortly after MAK fell apart. The collapse of MAK resulted in most of its members joining Bin Laden's new organization, al-Qaeda.

When Iraq invaded Kuwait in August of 1990, Osama

Bin Laden approached King Fahd to offer the services of his Mujahideen in an effort to help the vastly outnumbered Saudi forces. King Fahd rejected the offer and instead opted to allow the U.S. led Coalition Forces into Saudi Arabia to drive Saddam's forces from Kuwait. This decision angered Osama Bin Laden and he began publicly challenging the King. Osama thought it was disgraceful to allow the infidel forces to set foot upon the Holy Land. This feud resulted in Bin Laden being banished and forced into exile.

It was also during this time that the FBI began uncovering ties to Bin Laden's new organization in America. In November of 1990 the FBI raided the home of El Sayyid Nosair, an associate of Ali Mohammed.[10] During the raid they discovered plans to destroy buildings in New York City and Ali Mohammed was nowhere to be found. Although he was a Sergeant in the U.S. Army stationed at Fort Hood in North Carolina, Ali separated from the military and moved to California. He wasn't there for very long before he was off to Afghanistan. Ali Mohammed is said to have worked very closely with Bin Laden and also helped him to get situated in Sudan. In 1993 El Sayyid Nosair was convicted for the failed bombing of the World Trade Center.

Osama Bin Laden continued his verbal campaign of abuse against King Fahd until finally in 1994 the King sent an emissary to Sudan. The emissary was to demand Bin Laden's passport. At this time the King also revoked Osama's Saudi citizenship and demanded Bin Laden's family cut him off. It is estimated he was receiving about seven million dollars a month in allowance.[11] Osama's assets were frozen in Saudi Arabia and his family publically disowned him.

It is around this time that the Egyptian Islamic Jihad (EIJ) led by Ayman al-Zawahiri began making news with a botched attempt to assassinate the Prime Minister of Egypt, Atef Sedki, which resulted in the killing of a school girl.[12] This swayed Egyptian public opinion against the Islamist attacks and the government arrested 280 members of the group, executing 6 of them. This was a significant blow to the EIJ, organization renown for the assassination of Egyptian President Anwar Sadat in 1981. In June of 1995 another poorly executed attempt on the life of Egyptian President Mubarak resulted in the expulsion of EIJ and soon after, in 1996, also Bin Laden from Sudan. It is important to mention that on several occasions the Sudanese Government offered to hand Bin Laden over to the United States, but the opportunities were refused by the Clinton Administration National Security Advisor Sandy Berger, under the advice of Susan Rice and Richard Clarke.[13]

As we continue through this timeline I think it is important to recognize exactly how long this Jihad has been going on. It is essential to understand just how long these organizations have been scheming, plotting and attacking those deemed enemies of an emerging Islamic State. This idea is not a new concept and the Jihad we are now facing has been in existence in its present form for almost 50 years. We are witnessing the culmination of almost a half a century of war designed to establish a new Islamic State and caliphate.

Seven years after the Soviet withdrawal from Afghanistan the country remained ungoverned because of constant infighting until eventually an organization called the Taliban began to take form. The word Taliban literally means "Students," and history reveals an organization comprised of the beleaguered children of a 20 year war who have grown up on mountainous battlefields. The battle hardened veterans were educated in schools called "Madrassas," that were quickly established within the refugee camps along the Afghan-Pakistan borders.[14] The schools were mostly paid for by donations from wealthy Arabs, and indoctrinated its students in the hardline Salafi belief system.

The Salafi belief system is an extreme indoctrination of the Holy Qur'an as it was intended during the first generation, or medieval times. The word Salafi means "Early Muslim," and is used to refer to those born within the first 400 years of the Prophet Muhammad. Today the term is used to describe an ideology for those who want the return of sharia law. This belief system coupled with the hardships of growing up in a war-torn country is what produced the callus governing body of Afghanistan known as the Taliban.

It is important to note that the large donations received for the construction of refugee camps, schools and relief aid, were also the vehicles for supporters to channel revenue towards Bin Laden to fund operations. With the Taliban governing the country, bank deposits and money transfers were easily laundered to Osama. Al-Qaeda was able to operate within Afghanistan with impunity as long as the Taliban remained in control. Terrorists had the ability to travel to and from Afghanistan with no measure of accountability. Training camps were established, tactics were shared, and plans were being masterminded. Now it was time to present al-Qaeda to the world.

On August 7th 1998, car bombs explode simultaneously at the U.S. embassies in Nairobi, Kenya and Dar Es Salaam, Tanzania.[15] These coordinated attacks would kill 223 and injure over 4,000 in what would be the first joint effort between the Egyptian Islamic Jihad and al-Qaeda.[22] In response United States President Bill Clinton launched missile strikes into Afghanistan targeting the known terrorist training camps constructed by Bin Laden. The international community enforced sanctions on Afghanistan while U.S. officials demanded Osama Bin Laden be handed over. Taliban rule repeatedly ignored the requests. A new era of Jihad had arisen and the next attack would officially introduce al-Qaeda and awaken the world.

On September 11th 2001, nineteen al-Qaeda terrorists high jacked four passenger airplanes.[17] They intended to fly the airliners into four different targets, three out of the four hit their intended objectives. Two of the aircraft, United Airlines flight 175 and American Airlines flight 11 were flown into the World Trade Center buildings. American Airlines flight 77 was crashed into the Pentagon. The final jet, United Airlines flight 93, which was intended to strike a target in Washington D.C., instead crashed in a field outside Shanksville, Pennsylvania. The passengers of United Airlines flight 93 successfully overwhelmed the terrorists but were killed in the resulting crash. The events of 9/11 killed 2,996, injured countless others and changed America forever.

This particular terrorist strike proved to the world that America was indeed a nation that could be attacked on its own soil. In a video released on September 16th 2001, Osama Bin Laden said "The awakening of the Muslim umma (nation) has occurred."[18] On October 26th 2001, the "Patriot Act" would be signed into law by President George W. Bush, and the freedoms and rights of Americans would forever be altered. On December 18th 2001, for better or worse, congress would approve a measure to allow the president to designate September 11th "Patriot Day," a day we will never forget, a day believed by many to be the greatest victory in the current Jihad being waged by radical Islamic terrorists. That day would mark the day when many of the constitutional rights of American citizens were suspended because of fear of terrorism.

Shortly after the attacks on 9/11, President George W. Bush demanded that the Taliban regime in Afghanistan hand over Osama Bin Laden and expel al-Qaeda from its borders. The Taliban asked Bin Laden to leave but would not extradite him. In response the United States, with the help of the United Kingdom, launched Operation Enduring Freedom and invaded Afghanistan on October 7th 2001.[19] Operations in Afghanistan allowed the U.S. and its allies to establish military bases near almost every major town and city in the country. Allied forces would eventually cripple the Taliban and oust them from power. However the invasion would result in very few captured al-Qaeda and Taliban members as most fled to neighboring Pakistan.

Al-Qaeda, and the global Jihad it is waging, was now firmly rooted in the minds of every American. A country, still in shock over the devastation, was left to speculate what the next step would be? The people of America were being convinced weapons of mass destruction (WMDs) were in Iraq, and it was only a matter of time before they would be deployed on American soil. On March 19th 2003, the United States, backed by a patriotic fervor that the nation hasn't seen since World War II, proceeded with the invasion of Iraq. The war is kicked off with an airstrike on the Presidential Palace in Baghdad and the following day coalition forces moved into the Basra Province located close to the Iraq-Kuwait border. These events marked the beginning of a conflict that would entangle our nation with war for a period lasting longer than any other in our nation's history.

BORN OF CHAOS

The inception of the Islamic State can be traced back to the Second Gulf War, the invasion of Iraq in 2003. In response to 9/11, the United States and a coalition of nations invaded Iraq and toppled dictator Saddam Hussein. Toppling Saddam's regime seemed too easy and indeed it was. Our forces fought their way to the nation's capital with relative ease and there they were received by crowds of cheering Iraqis. Within three weeks Saddam's forces had been overrun and President Bush declared that the major ground fighting was complete and the Iraqi people had been liberated from a dictatorship.

Within hours the crowds that had gathered to celebrate the fall of Saddam's regime began looting. The ransacking was of such a large scale, the American forces chose not to interfere, allowing it to continue for days. The looting was not the response of a liberated people; it was the response of a people who believed there was no authority. They believed there was no authority in place to stop them, and they were correct. This lack of a governing presence was a dangerous oversight by the invading forces which had just sacked a nation.

The Bush administration, under the direction of Vice

President Dick Cheney, would select Ambassador L. Paul Bremer to help Iraq establish a democracy and institute a new government. Many did not feel he was the right choice to guide Iraq into democracy. Bremer did not speak Arabic and had little working knowledge of Middle Eastern customs and politics. Some believe that his lack of understanding in regards to middle eastern politics were exactly the reason he was chosen by Cheney. He would blindly follow the course set by Cheney and Donald Rumsfeld, Secretary of Defense.

Within the first week of Bremer's arrival in Iraq the Coalition Provisional Authority (CPA) Order No.1 would be introduced.[1] This would become known as the "De-ba'athification Order" and would end Sunni domination of the Iraqi government. By way of design it would also bring in rival ethnic and religious groups of Shi'ites to replace the Baathist Party. This order would begin driving the ruling Sunni Baathist Party out of power and into hiding. In retrospect this was a huge mistake, because it effectively removed the only people who knew how to govern and run the country, rendering them powerless. CPA Order No.1 not only removed Baathist Party members from government but also displaced teachers, engineers, doctors, police, security and military personal as well. This created immediate discontent from the Sunni population. It would be hard for me to imagine another country or entity here in America firing all the police, emergency responders, teachers and doctors, only to replace them all with possibly less qualified individuals. I think American Citizens affected by this displacement would be up in arms as well.

The second decision executed would be to dissolve the Iraqi military. When the majority of armed forces leaders were removed from position almost the entire military abandoned their posts taking their weapons with them. Several hundred thousand well-armed Sunnis who felt betrayed and powerless went into hiding and within 72 hours a car bomb went off at the Iraqi International Airport. Many would consider this the beginning of the real struggles in Iraq.

In the aftermath of operation Iraqi Freedom we saw the capture of Saddam Hussein.[2] Upon his capture he was turned over to a war time tribunal that found him guilty of crimes against humanity.[3] We handed the former Sunni leader over to a Shi'ite led government to be judged. He would be executed by way of hanging on December 30th 2006.[4]

We invaded Iraq, in part, because it was explained to us that the American government had irrefutable evidence that the Iraqi regime, under Saddam Hussein, possessed WMDs. It was also believed that they were harboring and working with known terrorists to plot more attacks on the United States. However contrary to popular belief, Saddam was actually an ally and even conferred with the United States Government before invading Kuwait in 1990.[5] When the United States began the troop buildup during Desert Shield, it was Saddam who felt betrayed.

Saddam Hussein had a history of working with the U.S. that dates back to 1958. In the mid-fifties during the Cold War era, Iraq joined the "Anti-Soviet Baghdad Pact."[6] Iraq was seen as a necessary buffer in the Middle East to prevent Soviet advancement. The pact required Iraq to defend the region's countries from Soviet attack. In 1958 the Iraqi Prime Minister, General Abd al-Karim Qasim seized power by overthrowing the ruling monarchy of Iraq.[7] Qasim quickly withdrew from the Anti-Soviet Baghdad Pact and began buying weapons and arms from the Soviet Union. This move quickly captured the attention of the CIA who noted that Qasim had begun placing known communist sympathizers into key positions within the newly formed government. At this point Iraq was perceived as one of the top threats in the world. It was then that the CIA began to work with the Egyptian intelligence agency, and was introduced to a 22 year old

Saddam Hussein. The CIA would authorize the assassination of Qasim and a six man team, that included Saddam Hussein, would be used for the operation. In 1959 Saddam and the other members of the team attempted to gun down Qasim on the streets of Baghdad. This first attempt in 1959 was a failure, as Qasim escaped with minor wounds. However another attempt in 1963 would prove successful, in what would become known as the Ba'ath Party Coup.[8] Qasim and anyone believed to be a part of the communist party were executed or imprisoned. It is believed the CIA had provided the list of communist sympathizers to be captured during the coup.

Saddam would become head of the al-Jihaz a-Khas, which was the secret intelligence agency of the Ba'ath Party. While in this position he would work closely with the CIA for many years until he eventually became the fifth President of Iraq on July 16th 1979.[9] While under Saddam's leadership the United States would provide Iraq with weapons and intelligence in an effort to support Iraq's involvement in the Iran Iraq War. Iraq and Saddam would remain a strong ally of the United States until the Iraq invasion of Kuwait on August 2nd 1990.

The attacks of 9/11 were not planned or perpetrated by Iraqi citizens. Iraq was not in possession of, nor did we find the weapons of mass destruction that we were told existed. I fought in Iraq and witnessed the devastation we levied on that country firsthand, I knew there were no weapons of mass destruction. Any capability to manufacture WMDs was obliterated during the first Gulf War. However our presence certainly accelerated the learning curve and created the chaotic environment required to produce battle-hardened extremist fighters and organizations.

The fighting forces of the infidels occupying Iraq and Afghanistan was enough to focus the efforts of multiple extremist groups, which we began referring to as insurgents. Although the insurgency groups fighting coalition forces and the new Iraqi government were diverse, it appeared to be led by the extremist Islamic group al-Qaeda. This is when multiple Islamic terrorist groups begin flocking to the al-Qaeda banner.

At the time al-Qaeda efforts in Iraq were being led by Abu Musab al-Zarqawi. In 2004 he was chosen by Bin Laden to lead the al-Qaeda efforts in Iraq.[10] Al-Zarqawi swore his allegiance to Osama and was given the title "Emir of al-Qaeda in the Country of Two Rivers." He was a Jordanian Islamist militant who was the leader of the Islamist terrorist group al-Tawhid wal-Jihad. He became well known for his savage beheadings of American hostages Nick Berg and Eugene Armstrong. He is said to be the man in the mask standing directly behind and beheading each man in the videos. He also masterminded multiple bombings and vicious attacks on military, civilian and government targets during the Iraq War. After an Iraqi government led assault on the insurgents in the town of Tal Afar in 2005, al-Zarqawi began a full scale assault on the Shi'ites in Iraq. He created mayhem for the coalition forces and the newly formed Iraqi government until his death in 2006.

Although al-Zarqawi's leadership role in al-Qaeda was brief, it is important to mention. It was under his leadership that we see much of the tactics now being used by the Islamic State. Al-Zarqawi had realized the importance of an important new tool and started integrating social media into his campaign of terror. The ruthless beheadings, attacks on police stations, government buildings, and military recruiting stations were all videotaped and used as important propaganda material to recruit others to his cause in Iraq via the internet.

These same tactics are now being duplicated and employed on a much larger scale by the Islamic State of Iraq. Because of social media we are witnessing firsthand the slaughter of thousands. During the month of June in 2014, IS militants posted horrific images and videos using the hashtag "#worldcup" to spread their terror to those following the World Cup soccer games.[11] Social media has granted the world access to view the execution of hundreds of military recruits, mass beheadings, bombings, drive by shootings, and countless other acts of terror. The world witnessed attacks on large-scale prisons releasing thousands of inmates to join the ranks of the Islamic State's murderous horde. The selective attacks killing government officials are recorded and used to raise awareness for recruiting campaigns. Long after allegiance is pledged and strict sharia law is established they continue filming the strong-arm tactics to discourage future resistance. As the cameras continue to film these ruthless acts we begin to see the role social media has played in the evolution of both terror and war.

The fighting would continue in Iraq and the hunt for Bin Laden would continue in Afghanistan until finally the moment the world anticipated arrived. On May 2nd 2011, a CIA led operation entitled Neptune's Spear was launched. Bin Laden's whereabouts were confirmed and a U.S. Special Warfare Development Group (Navy Seal Team 6) was dispatched to capture or kill Osama Bin Laden. On that night in Pakistan Osama Bin Laden was killed.[12] This would end a manhunt for the most wanted man on the planet that lasted nearly a decade.

There would be no evidence of the execution of Bin Laden. We would not be shown his body. There would be no formal trial. There would be no public execution. There would be no burial; his body would be put to rest in the middle of the ocean in an undisclosed location. There were many uncertainties surrounding the death of Osama Bin Laden, but we celebrated as a nation nonetheless and declared another victory in the war on terror.

His death seemed to coincide with a sharp decline in the terrorist attacks in Iraq and throughout the region. For a brief period it seemed as if the war on terror was actually gaining ground. So with the death of Osama Bin Laden amidst the heat of a campaign for re-election, President Obama announced the timeline for withdrawal of U.S. forces from Iraq and Afghanistan. What we did not know at the time was that we were witnessing the calm before the storm.

Osama Bin Laden's death was seen by many as a weakening of al-Qaeda and the U.S. began to see certain Islamic factions splinter in an attempt to seize power. This is not uncommon and usually creates some infighting within the Islamic groups as leaders vie for position to claim a successor. The brief period of posturing and infighting quieted the region even more as the leaders continued to plot ascension rather than revenge. In the wake of Osama Bin Laden's death Ayman al-Zawahiri was named the successor to lead al-Qaeda.[13] This move came as no surprise to those who understood the hierarchy of al-Qaeda. Eventually, a more extreme leader would emerge from one of the splintering factions who would go on to challenge the authority of Ayman al-Zawahiri to lead.

Abu Bakr al-Baghdadi was the leader of the branch of al-Qaeda in Iraq. He was the man in charge when the last of the U.S. troops withdrew on December 18th 2011. With no coalition forces to depend on, Iraq's security forces were left to defend the Shi'ite formed government. The Sunni's, although significantly outnumbering the Shi'ite Muslims in Iraq, had for the most part been excluded from the decision making process and held virtually no leverage in the new government. This proved to be the catalyst needed to recruit fighters to al-Qaeda's cause in Iraq. Ayman al-Zawahiri had been patient long enough and instructed the al-Qaeda branch in Iraq to once again begin ramping up the attacks on the Shi'ite dominated government.

Suicide attacks began targeting police, military, and government buildings, and with the renewed aggressions of al-Qaeda, the Iraqi Government and Security Force began crumbling. The improved success of the assaults inspired Sunni militants from all over the Middle East to join the fight against the Shi'ite dominated regime in Iraq. With the influx of Islamic Sunni fighters flocking to the region, Abu Bakr al-Baghdadi changed the name of the al-Qaeda branch in Iraq to the Islamic State of Iraq (ISI).

The troop withdrawal, renewed attacks, and birth of the Islamic State in Iraq, was overshadowed by an event that became known as the "Arab Spring."[14] What started in Tunisia spread across the desert like a hot wind to Egypt, Libya, Jordan, Yemen, Bahrain, Morocco, Syria, Saudi Arabia, Sudan, Oman, Palestine and Jerusalem. This event began in December of 2010 with demonstrations, protests, civil uprisings, labor strikes, and even the declaration of civil war. Although it went almost unnoticed to the Western World it eventually sparked an event known as the "January 25th Revolution." What began as protests in Egypt, eventually tuned into a revolution capturing the world's attention.

Egypt had been under Emergency Law (Martial Law) since 1967 when it was enacted after the Six-Day War of Israel.[15] Since 1968 the Emergency Law No.162 had been in effect, with the exception of once briefly during the early 80s. After the assassination of Anwar Sadat in 1981 the Emergency Law was quickly reinstated and had remained in effect ever since. Shortly after the assassination of Sadat, Muhammad Hosni El Sayed Mubarak took over as the 4th President of Egypt, and ruled for over thirty years by maintaining a Police State under the Emergency Law.

It was this Police State that was Mubarak's eventual undoing, as police brutality was one of the main reasons for the demonstrations that eventually turned into a full scale revolution. It is interesting to note the recent public reaction to police brutality within the United States, very similar public gatherings and demonstrations have been taking place. Under the Emergency Law in Egypt, police powers were extended, constitutional rights were suspended, and *Habeas Corpus* was abolished. The choice to enact the emergency law was made as a result of terrorist attacks and assassination attempts. It was feared that without the police state the Muslim Brotherhood would be able to thrive and dictate the democratic government. Either way it was fear of terrorists that enabled one man to call himself President of a democratic society for over thirty years.

These are very important observations which deserve our attention. It is essential for us to recognize when another democratic government has been turned into a dictatorship by enforcing a police state or martial law. It is not that difficult to draw parallels of our own government, which growing opinion believes is slipping into a police state. What will be the trigger to enact martial law within the United States? Will it be a terrorist attack? Who will assume command while the government and our liberties are suspended? Are we willing to surrender our constitutional rights because of fear? I think Benjamin Franklin understood the nature of freedom when he said "Those who surrender freedom for security will not have, nor do they deserve, either one."

After the demonstrations in Egypt led to a regime change demanded by the people, a similar uprising began in Syria. However, the demonstrations in Syria quickly accelerated to violent clashes as the al-Assad regime countered the resistance with brutal force. This created sympathy within the region and caused large numbers of the regime to defect and form the Free Syrian Army (FSA). The FSA began attracting sympathizers to the rebellion and Syria erupted into civil war.

Shortly after the war the United States started overtly and covertly supplying weapons and resources to the rebels which intensified the fighting in Syria.[16] In an effort to expand his war Abu Bakr al-Baghdadi devised a plan to exploit the Sunni Shia animosity and in 2011 he sends one of his most experienced fighters Abu Mohammed al-Jolani to Syria. This move was to establish a new branch of al-Qaeda in the wake of the Syrian civil war. As a result Abu Mohammed al-Jolani, who calls Syria his homeland, was quickly able to establish a large resistance network called the al-Nusra Front.

The al-Nusra Front led by al-Jolani rapidly became recognized as the largest and most effective rebel force in Syria and fought side by side with the FSA. These are the rebels that President Obama pledged support to. His promise led many active duty armed forces members in the United States to take to social media saying they would not support or contribute to the backing of the Syrian rebels who were partly comprised of al-Qaeda Islamic terrorists. This caused the United States to then parley the United Nations to provide support for the Syrian rebels in their fight against Bashar al-Assad the nation's President.

Meanwhile after the success of the al-Nusra Front in Syria, Abu Bakr al-Baghdadi, expecting the loyalty of al-Jolani, changed the Islamic State of Iraq (ISI) to the Islamic State of Iraq and Syria, or ISIS.[17] The fighting in Iraq continued to intensify and ISIS delivered devastating blows to the Iraqi Security Forces. With the Iraqi military faltering, ISIS claimed large chunks of land as it continued to take over and occupy cities, towns, villages and provinces throughout Iraq and Syria. This had not been achieved by any modern day Islamic militant groups. The successes began attracting Sunni Islamic militants from around the world and ISIS's numbers began to swell.

However Abu Mohammed al-Jolani did not want to pledge the allegiance of his Syrian born freedom fighters to the Islamic State of Iraq and renounced his ties to Abu Bakr al-Baghdadi.[18] Al-Jolani wanted to create a separate Islamic State in Syria under the control of al-Qaeda. Al-Jolani then turned to Ayman al-Zawahiri the leader of al-Qaeda who instructed al-Baghdadi to dissolve the Islamic State of Iraq and Syria and refocus his efforts on Iraq.[19] This was the equivalent of a king governing a feudal system who set two feuding warlords against each other to settle their dispute.

When al-Baghdadi refused to abandon his efforts to create a caliphate for the Islamic State, Ayman al-Zawahiri publicly announced that al-Qaeda was renouncing ties to ISIS.[20] This is when al-Baghdadi instructed ISIS fighters to engage al-Nusra, who at the time, were embroiled in combat with the al-Assad Regime. This move dealt a heavy blow to the FSA and al-Nusra with some estimates saying up to 80% of their numbers defected to ISIS.[21]

With the numbers swelling in Syria it was time for another name change as the Islamic State dropped Syria from its moniker and replaced it with Levant, the Islamic State of Iraq and Levant (ISIL).[22] Levant refers to a historical geographical reference to a large portion of Southwest Asia that encompasses not only Syria but also Cypress, Hatay, Jordan, Lebanon, Palestine, Egypt, Turkey and Israel. This should be a clear indicator of the future plans for the Islamic State.

With this move ISIL begins operations in Syria killing almost indiscriminately while forcing tribal leaders and supporters of the FSA and al-Nusra to swear allegiances to ISIL. As of January 2015 the Islamic State is in control of over a third of Syria. It has more than doubled its area of control in just a few short months despite over 1,300 airstrikes into ISIL controlled areas.[23] The Islamic State now controls, not only the entire Syria-Iraq border, but also has added the major cities of Raqqa, Tabqah and Aleppo to its caliphate.

The Islamic State, born out of chaos, has now become the wealthiest, most powerful and brutal terrorist organization in the world. They control more weapons and firepower than any previous terrorist organization ever. The Islamic State is a serious threat and it appears as if a clash is inevitable, they deserve our complete attention. The countdown has begun.

THE MAN IN BLACK

Clad in a black turban and dark priestly robes he had the unassuming appearance of an Imam as he stepped forth with the chants of Allah Akbar (God is Great) ringing out around him. Sunlight shone in through the ornate walls and fixtures of the mosque as he climbed the stairs and approached the microphone. Silence fell over the crowd gathered for prayer on that holy day as he began to address the people before him.

In a grandiose manner the choices made were designed to invoke the early Islamic empire and its leadership. He chose the first prayer Friday of Ramadan to come forth. He chose the recently conquered mosque in Mosul to give his speech. He chose this setting to announce the declaration of the Islamic Caliphate and urged Muslims everywhere to join in Jihad. With a holy fervor he reminded everyone that Ramadan is a month to wage Jihad, and a time when the prophet built armies to fight the enemies of God. He stepped from the shadows and proclaimed himself the Caliph of the Caliphate of the Islamic State, and in doing so declared that he was now the leader of the entire Muslim world.[1] His name is Abu Bakr Al-Baghdadi, a name the world will not soon forget.

Al-Baghdadi's real name is Ibrahim Awwad Ibrahim Ali al-Badri, but he is also known as Abu Awad or Abu Dua (Dua being the name of his eldest daughter) and The Ghost.[2] He has been called The Ghost because he is very secretive and moves in a clandestine manner, rarely allowing himself to be filmed or photographed. On the rare occasions when The Ghost named Abu Bakr al-Baghdadi is seen in public, he is always surrounded by a large heavily armed security force.

It is said that he was born in 1971 in a place located in the Sunni-triangle north of Baghdad called Samarra. He is believed to have come from the al-Jibriya district, a lower-middle-class sector controlled by the Albu Badri and the Albu Baz tribes. This area was hit particularly hard, being heavily bombed and patrolled by U.S. forces, after the invasion in 2003.

A self-proclaimed caliph, who now controls parts of Iraq and Syria, his voice commands thousands. People who remember the man behind ISIS say he was a quiet studious boy without many friends. It is said that his time was spent in mosques, reading books and attending religious courses as a child.[3] It is presumed that al-Baghdadi, at or around the age of 18, would have performed some military service. This probably provided him with at least limited exposure to weapon use and basic military tactics. It is also rumored that he was tutored in his studies of the Holy Qur'an and the Hadith (traditions, deeds and sayings of the prophet Muhammad), by two renowned clerics, Sheikh Subhi al-Saarai and Sheikh Adnan al-Ameen, both of whom are now deceased.[4] Al-Baghdadi is also said to have received a Ph.D. in religious studies and is reported to have preached at the Great Mosque in Baghdad as well as the Ahmad ibn Hanbal Mosque in Samarra. However much of what is known about al-Baghdadi is hard to verify as most of his family and known associates have gone into hiding for fear of retaliation for his horrific actions.

The ruthless tactics and horrors perpetrated by ISIS are a direct result of al-Baghdadi's leadership. After the US led forces toppled Saddam Hussein's regime the country soon fell into chaos. Those Sunni who remained behind began their vicious assaults against the U.S. led forces and this is where the insurgency started. Most agree al-Baghdadi helped to establish the terrorist group Jamaat Jaish Ahl al-Sunnah wal Jamaa which claimed responsibility for a myriad of car bombings and suicide attacks in Iraq.[5] In an attempt to capture high value targets the U.S. led forces launched a sweeping campaign to cripple the insurgency efforts. The particularly violent Jordanian terrorist believed to be an al-Qaeda mastermind in Iraq, Abu Musab al-Zarqawi, was one of the main targets of these efforts. During this campaign al-Baghdadi was captured in 2005.[6]

After his capture in 2005 al-Baghdadi was held at Camp Bucca, a detention facility located in southern Iraq near Umm Qasr. Although he had been suspected of terrorist activities he could not be linked to any. It was believed but never confirmed that al-Baghdadi was in some way connected to al-Zarqawi.

It is uncertain exactly how long he remained in this detention camp, but it is believed this is where he established many contacts and shared information regarding al-Qaeda and future terrorist plots. Many terrorist and Ba'athists party leaders passed through this camp. Ideas and ideals were shared freely with one another directly under coalition supervision. There are many who believe that it was during this time in captivity that al-Baghdadi was exposed to the idea and the planning of the future Islamic State of Iraq. He is quoted by senior officials as saying "see you in New York" upon being released from the detention facility.[7]

Although al-Baghdadi met and was probably tutored by al-Qaeda operatives during his captivity in Camp Bucca, it wasn't until 2010 that he assumed a leadership role within the organization. It was in mid-2010 that Abu Omar al-

Baghdadi, or Hamed al-Zawi, was killed.[8] Abu Omar al-Baghdadi was believed to be the leader of the Iraqi branch of al-Qaeda which was operating under the name Islamic State of Iraq (ISI). However there is speculation that Abu Omar al-Baghdadi was a fabricated persona, created to fool western forces by giving a false face and name to the leadership of the Iraqi branch of al-Qaeda.[9] Upon the real or fictitious death of Omar al-Baghdadi, Abu Bakr al-Baghdadi assumed the role of leader. At this point the ISI was collapsing and much of the secular violence had subsided significantly compared to previous years. When the U.S. withdrew troops from Iraq in 2011 Abu Bakr al-Baghdadi seized the opportunity and began a new wave of strategically targeted terrorist attacks designed to weaken the Iraqi Security Forces and Shi'ite dominated fledgling government.

Abu Bakr al-Baghdadi was now in complete control of the terrorist insurgency in Iraq and ISI was again on the offensive. This would mark the beginning of some of the most horrifying acts of terrorism the planet has ever seen. Not only would the Middle East never be the same again, but neither would the world.

CALIPHATE

When the phone at my desk rang I just stared at it for a moment while contemplating whether or not I should pick it up. I hadn't been myself this morning after what I had seen. I just couldn't seem to shake the images from my mind. As I pulled away from the driveway this morning I could see people coming out of their homes. It was then I noticed the small crowd in front of Rick's house. It took me a second to make him out, but eventually I saw Rick. He was tied to the tree in his front yard with no shirt on. Rick had been my neighbor for fifteen years and I simply couldn't believe what I was seeing, so I pulled back up into my drive way and I got out of the car. As I slowly started walking towards my neighbor's house I began counting the men surrounding Rick and came up with ten. While I was counting one of the men stepped forward and began reading out loud Rick's offense against the state, followed by a prescribed punishment.

Rick was to begin his first set of weekly lashes for banned content found on his computer. He was beginning his first 25 lashes on his way to 1,000. He would be whipped every week for a little over a year as his punishment for posting and accessing inappropriate material on the internet.

I can still see the pain that ran across his face as the first of the 25 lashes were being handed out. I forced myself to stay and watch as the punishment was being administered. I could see the crowd wince in anticipation and gasp with each delivery of the whip. It was another twisted reminder of the sad state of affairs we were currently in. Since the declaration of Sharia law we have all felt the whip in one way or another.

Again the ringing phone snaps my attention back to the present and I quickly reach for the receiver. "Hello.." I say into the phone. "Yes," I repeat, answering every question thrown at me, "of course, I will be right there." It takes a second for the information to settle in. All I knew for certain was I had to go pick my son up from his school. I explain to my boss that I have to go and will be back as soon as I can.

On the drive over to the school I replay the phone call in my mind one more time in an effort to make sense of what I heard. From what I could gather, before school the kids were outside playing beyond the barriers on the edge of the abandoned buildings gathering stones. The stones being gathered were to be used later for the stoning of a woman who committed adultery. The woman being stoned has a son the same age as my son and they are friends. My son listened to the boys laughing and joking as they searched for perfect stones to be cast at his friend's mother. My son abandoned the search for stones upon learning who they were going to be used on and went back to school.

I learned from his teacher that later, when the stoning was announced in class and chosen as a topic of discussion, my son got upset and told the class he wouldn't participate. It is now being suggested that he be forced to attend and participate in the stoning of his friends mother.

During the meeting at the school I am instructed to take my son and prepare him for participation in the public stoning to be held later that night. I am also informed that our names have been given to the State Information Bureau for follow up interviews. I nod in agreement and when we are through being instructed I walk my son out of the building. I hold his hand and ponder what the next steps will be. Life has become difficult while being governed under sharia law. Giving his hand an extra squeeze I look down through a cloud of doubt and ask him, "Where do we go to find stones my son?"

One should consider if that is what it would be like to live in a caliphate? Would I have to take my son to gather stones for public executions? I often try to imagine what a typical day might look like being governed by sharia law? I think these are the types of questions more people should be asking themselves, because the ultimate goal of the Islamic State is suggested in the name itself. We are witnessing the development of a religious police state. In addition to hearing about ISIS, ISIL or IS, you have probably heard the word caliphate mentioned as well.

A caliphate is a form of Islamic government. It is the goal of the Islamic State to create this Islamic government for the Muslim world. The caliphate is not a nation so it does not recognize international law. A caliphate is governed by sharia law alone. This is important to remember as we continue to examine the caliphate established by IS. The Islamic State is creating an all-encompassing caliphate to include and represent the entire Muslim population around the world. By establishing a caliphate the Islamic State has shown the world it is returning to the old ways and has elevated its status above all others in the eyes of Muslims.

The world caliph means "successor" and is used to designate the political and religious leader of the Islamic community. This reference to community is meant to encompass or include all Muslims around the globe. By claiming the title of Caliph, Abu Bakr al-Baghdadi has declared himself the successor to the Prophet Muhammad and ruler of the entire Muslim world. According to Abu Bakr al-Baghdadi, his word is the word of God and he is calling on all "true" Muslims to support the Caliph and the five pillars of Islam. This is a scary thought to think that this murdering leader of the Islamic State has now declared himself the leader of all 1.5 billion Muslims around the world. Within days of announcing the creation of the Caliphate of the Islamic State to the world, he urged other militant groups and Muslims around the globe to join him.[1] He declared the need for doctors, scholars, judges, fuqaha (experts in Islamic jurisprudence), engineers and other administrative experts to help maintain the caliphate. "Therefore, rush, o Muslims to your state. Yes, it is your state. Rush because Syria is not for the Syrians, Iraq is not for the Iraqis. The earth is Allah's." he said in a distributed audio statement.[2] Al-Baghdadi's strategy requires him to continue capitalizing on the victories as more and more flock to the black banner of IS daily.

In order to better understand a caliphate, we will look into the past and examine one of the earliest caliphates. The Umayyad Caliphate was the second of the four major caliphates and was established in the 7th century.[3] Soon after the Prophet Muhammad's death Abu Bakr al-Siddiq was declared Caliph of the caliphate.[4] This is one of the major disagreements between the Shi'ite and Sunni Muslims. The Shi'ite believe that Ali should have been chosen as caliph because he was a blood relative of Prophet Mohammed. Although al-Siddiq was not directly related to the Prophet Muhammad, the Sunni Muslims chose him because he was an advisor to the Prophet and a strong religious leader. The Sunnis believed it was more important to be a strong leader, and the title of "Caliph" should not be limited to succession of bloodline only. It is these religious differences that inspire the cries of jihad and acts of terror that continue to plague the world to this very day.

The Umayyad Caliphate, at its height covered 5.8 million square miles of the Arabian Peninsula and was, at the time, the largest empire the world had ever seen.[5] The most recent caliphate existed for over 500 years and lasted until 1923 when Turkey established their own republic and broke away from the Ottoman Empire at the end of World War I. This caused the caliphate to collapse under pressure from western civilizations and the ruling Sultan and Caliph lost power and were soon only recognized by title. Due to a growing power struggle the caliph was eventually driven into hiding under persecution. This was a victory for the western world as the Ottoman Empire was no more and much of the Middle East was carved up and redistributed by the European nations. This dissolving of the Islamic caliphate and the abolishment of the caliph was described as a triumph that left the Islamic world and the Middle East leaderless.

As we observe and compare the caliphate of today with the ones from the past it is important to remember that the caliphate recognizes no borders. For the Islamic State to establish a caliphate in today's modern era, which relies heavily on borders and economics, is an incredible accomplishment. When we examine the intricate infrastructures created by countries through the use of borders, economics and governing tactics, we can then appreciate the force used to erase borders, topple infrastructures and eradicate ideologies in pursuit of a vision called the Islamic State.

Understanding the difference between the Sunni and Shi'ite Muslims helps to recognize the importance of this new caliphate being established in the Middle East. It is apparent that an ancient divide between the Sunni and Shi'ite Muslims continues to fuel a resurgence of hatred that threatens the stability of the Middle East and possibly the world. This great divide has recently contributed to the civil war that now plagues Syria and has fractured yet another country further destabilizing the Middle East. We can now see Yemen, Egypt, Lebanon and Libya being destabilized under civil war and Islamic extremism. Jordan appears to be next and will soon begin to destabilize due to pressure being applied by extremists.

With the entire Middle East erupting into turmoil, what is it that makes a Sunni Muslim and a Shi'ite Muslim so different that they are willing to turn their countries inside out? The Sunni Muslims are estimated to account for 85% to 90% of the Muslim population around the world, and are considered the more traditional or orthodox branch of Islam.[6] The word Sunni is derived from the phrase "Ahl al-Sunna" which translated means "the people of tradition." The estimates of Shi'ite Muslims are between 120-170 million globally which accounts for about 10% of all Muslims.[7] The Shi'ite name comes from the phrase "Shiat Ali" which means "the party of Ali." This was derived to show their loyalty to the lineage of the Prophet Muhammad by remaining loyal to Ali and the bloodline of the Prophet Muhammad.

The difference between the two comes down to understanding the lineage of the Prophet Muhammad. As we briefly discussed earlier the Prophet Muhammad established the religion of Islam in the seventh century and in 622 he founded the first Islamic State in the city of Medina located in western Saudi Arabia north of Mecca. It was in that same year that he gathered an army of 10,000 Muslims and captured the city of Mecca.[8]

The Prophet Muhammad never named a successor and when he died in 632, a great debate arose as to who should succeed him as caliph of the caliphate. Should he be replaced by someone of his bloodline, or should he be replaced by a candidate most likely to adhere to the tenets of the faith? The Sunni group agreed the caliph should be the prophet's first advisor and chose Abu Bakr to become the first successor of the Prophet Muhammad.[9] It was believed the advisor to the prophet would be a strong choice to lead the Muslim State. The Shi'ites instead favored Ali, the Prophet Muhammad's cousin and son-in-law. The Shi'ites believed the successor should be of the Prophet Muhammad's bloodline. Those who share a direct bloodline or are descendants of the Prophet Muhammad and Ali are called Imams. It is the Imams that are chosen to lead the Shi'ites. So the Sunni's chose Abu Bakr to become caliph of the caliphate and the Shi'ites chose an Imam to lead them.

After the 11th Imam died in 874 his young son was said to have disappeared from the funeral. Shi'ites came to revere this boy as a messiah that was chosen by God and hidden from the world until the day of his return. This is the belief of the largest sect of Shi'ites known as the "Twelver's" who have been preparing for his return ever since. The Sunnis believe the messiah has yet to come.

The Muslim world chose to settle its differences by their own accord and things remained relatively peaceful but only for a short period of time. In 656 Shi'ite supporters of Ali killed the third Caliph and in retaliation the Sunni's killed Ali's son Hussein. The fighting continued until eventually the Sunnis emerged victorious over the Shi'ites. The Shi'ites remained diligent and continued to develop their religious beliefs through their imams. The Sunni believed in the strength and prosperity of the caliphate and showed their devotion by remaining fiercely loyal to the caliph.

The Sunni appointed caliphs remained in power ruling the caliphate and the Arab world until the fall of the Ottoman Empire. I mention this again because this historical event was considered disastrous by the Sunni Muslims who revered the caliphate. This understanding sheds light on the current Sunni struggle for domination in the Middle East and their quest to reestablish a caliphate. They are literally trying to erase borders and restore the caliphate to the days of old at the height of the Ottoman Empire. They believe the western culture has not only robbed them of their caliphate, but also tainted their religious beliefs and weakened each successive generation since the collapse of the Caliphate of the Ottoman Empire.

What was considered a difference of religious opinion can now be seen as a secular divide that shows up in politics all across the Middle East. As we continue to examine the differences of Sunni and Shi'ite Muslims we must look at the secular divide in countries across the Middle East. Shi'ite Muslims are believed to be in the majority in Iraq, Iran, Bahrain, Yemen and Azerbaijan. Looking at the current crisis taking place in Syria and Iraq we find that both have Shi'ite dominated governments.

Although Sunni Muslims dominate Syria the al-Assad regime has aligned with Shi'ite dominated Iran.[10] This alignment has fueled the Sunni led revolution of Syria and has given IS an opportunity to grow in popularity in regions outside of Syria. The recent beheadings of Egyptians in Libya have demonstrated how quickly this discontent is capable of spreading.[11]

The Iraqi government was run by president Nuri Kemal al-Maliki, and is also a Shi'ite dominated government.[12] This difference once again provides the Sunni with reason to wage war. Many of the Sunni population of Iraq have viewed the Iraqi military as a strong-arm of the Shi'ite run government. This is one of the reasons that the Islamic State has been so successful in Iraq. Anything that opposes the Shi'ite dominated government will be held in popular regard by the Sunni population of Iraq. It becomes increasingly apparent that all the Islamic State has to do is align itself with Shi'ite opposing organizations and an instant foothold is achieved.

The Iranian revolution in 1979 and the radical Shi'ite agenda were perceived as a threat to Sunni Regimes throughout the Middle East. The rise to power of the Ayatollah Khomeini and the establishment of the world's first Islamic Republic State was seen by the Shi'ite population as the return of a legitimate religious figure.[13] This threat was perceived to be so great by the Sunni that it prompted Iraq to invade Iran in 1980 under the Saddam Hussein led regime.[14] The U.S. supported this move and considered Saddam an ally. The attack on the U.S. embassy in Iran and the hostage situation that resulted had deteriorated U.S. relations with Iran severely, that is until recently. It seems as if Iran is beginning to recognize the threat posed by the Islamic State. Iran recently began dialog with the United States regarding its nuclear program.[15] However most believe the talks to be a ruse to get the U.S. and U.N. to make a larger commitment to the war with the Islamic State. All the same these recent talks do reveal that Iran understands the Islamic State poses a very real threat to its Shi'ite population. The country recognizes that they are surrounded by radical Islamic militants and it is only a matter of time before the fight is brought to them.

CAUSE AND EFFECT

We have examined what the Islamic State is, their origins, goals, and we have identified who leads them. In addition we have also discussed factors that motivate them to do the things they do. Now we must examine their cause and the effect it is having on the rest of the world. They believe that they are transforming the Muslim world by reestablishing the old way of life and laws which have dictated and governed their faith for centuries. They have established a cause that has attracted Muslims from around the world to join in and support them. They are determined and their actions have shown just how resolute they are. They want the world to understand that they are not governed by established law. They are governed by their interpretation of their faith, the word of the caliph and sharia law only. They will continue committing atrocities upon fellow man because it would seem they have adopted a simple philosophy: if you are not with them you are against them, Muslim or not.

It is important to recognize that the Islamic State has been ruthless in its efforts to fulfill the agenda it has set. Since the Islamic State has turned its attention to creating a caliphate, they have been able to claim a significant portion of the Middle East and erase borders in the process. They have taken over cities and even control a dam, that many fear will be used to flood a major portion of Iraq.[1] IS has acquired military vehicles, tanks, anti-aircraft weapons, heavy weapons, light weapons, munitions, artillery and equipment of all kinds. They are also in control of a chemical manufacturing plant that many believe is being used to manufacture weapons of mass destruction.[2] They have raided banks, schools, prisons, hospitals and universities. They have continued to develop and institute their caliphate as the world watches seemingly powerless to stop them. Nowhere, no one, and nothing is off limits in their pursuit of establishing the Caliphate of the Islamic State.

Even the Suez Canal has come under assault recently as attacks have threatened all types of ships using the canal for passage. At one point Islamic State militants even managed to seize control of an Egyptian warship.[3] Because of the implications of capturing a warship this event garnered very little media attention. Four boats attacked an Egyptian naval vessel after it had come to a stop in response to a staged accident within the Suez Canal. Machine guns and rockets were fired at the naval vessel as the four boats closed in on the ship. Men began boarding and seized control of the vessel. Eventually the ship was retaken when naval ships and helicopters responded to recapture the ship. The attacking boats were destroyed and 38 men who boarded the naval vessel were apprehended. Make no mistake, this is unprecedented and never before has a terrorist organization been able to seize control of a warship. This is not the Somali pirates capturing cruise ships or freighters; this is the capture of a warship.

It is believed the plan was to capture a naval vessel carrying surface to air and surface to ground missiles to launch an attack into Israel and Egypt. It is certain the Suez Canal will be a strategic target and will soon have the full attention of the Islamic State as it continues to wage war. Control of those shipping lanes will certainly have an impact on the global economy.

The dangers that the Islamic State pose to the rest of the world are significant. It is estimated that the Islamic State has acquired over 88 pounds of uranium from research facilities and universities plundered in Iraq.[4] It is certainly conceivable that they already have people working on dirty bombs to be used in western countries such as, Great Britain and the United States. It is rumored that there are already people in position just waiting for the go ahead from the Caliph to initiate operations in Iran, Canada, Australia, Spain, South East Asia, China, Europe, Russia and America. It is almost certain there will be more chilling days ahead as we have only seen the beginning of what the Islamic State is capable of.

As the Islamic State continues to gain ground in the Middle East we will see more Islamic terrorist groups and organizations pledge their allegiance to the IS. As of February 15th 2015, we have seen numerous terrorist organizations, especially in northern Africa, pledge their allegiance to the Islamic State. Here is a list of some of the recent Islamic Terrorist groups that have pledged allegiance to the Islamic State.

Boko-Haram (Nigeria) This is a particularly dangerous group led by Abu Bakr Shekau. Boko-Haram is responsible for killing over 10,000 people in 2014 and on Jan 3rd 2015, the group assaulted the town of Baga killing over 2,000.[5] The city of Baga is located in northeastern Nigeria, and was attacked by the Islamic militant group resulting in the slaughter of over 2,000 innocent people. Most of the victims killed were woman, children, and the elderly who were slower escaping. They indiscriminately gunned down people in the streets and burned houses and buildings to the ground while people hid within them. Thousands of homes and structures were burnt to the ground in the attack as the group assumed control of the region. In a video released on YouTube Abu Bakr Shekau stated that God told him to slaughter the people of Baga and stated that this was just the tip of the iceberg in regards to the killings to come.[6] The group has bombed, raped, murdered and kidnapped in order to establish a caliphate in Nigeria.

Jund al-Khilafah, Soldiers of the Caliphate (North Africa) This organization is a break away or splinter group from the North African al-Qaeda affiliate. On September 14th 2014, Jund al-Khilafah leader announces that they are breaking away from al-Qaeda and swears allegiance to Abu Bakr al-Baghdadi.[7] Ten days later the group released a video in which they behead a 55 year-old French mountaineering guide.[8] This heinous crime was in response to Islamic State spokesperson al-Adnani who told followers of the Islamic State to attack citizens of foreign countries aligned with the U.S.

Ansar al-Shariah (Libya) This is a violent Islamic militant group that was formed during the Libyan Civil war and rose to power after the killing of Muammar Gaddafi. This group also participated in the 2012 Benghazi attacks which destroyed the American Diplomatic Compound and claimed the lives of several Americans, including U.S. Ambassador, J. Christopher Stevens, the first U.S. Ambassador killed on duty since 1979.[9] The leader of the group, Mohammed al-Zahawi, has stated that their goal is to help establish the caliphate of the Islamic State to be governed by Sharia law.[10] After organizing a demonstration of over 200 vehicles with mounted weapons, Mohammed al-Zahawi went on television and forbid people from taking part in the parliamentary elections being held in post revolution

Libya. The group also carried out the destruction of the Sufi Shrines in Benghazi, acts that were described as disgraceful by the General National Congress.[11] When the government began to push back in 2014 Ansar al-Shariah convinced other militant Islamic groups to rally and actually managed to capture several military bases seizing a considerable amount of weapons and ammunition.

Taliban (Afghanistan) The notorious Taliban has aligned with the Islamic State and has been actively recruiting for them. Several of the Taliban leaders released from Guantanamo Bay, by President Obama, have accepted large roles in both recruiting and training for the Islamic State.[12] It is evident by the tactics and indiscriminant executions of civilians for not adhering to strict Sharia Law the Islamic State has adopted the Taliban's hardline tactics. It is clearly stated by the killing of more than 130 children at the school in Peshawar, Pakistan, that the Taliban is aligned with IS in its campaign of terror.[13] On December 16th 2014, Taliban Islamic militant terrorists went from building to building, room to room, opening fire on students and teachers. The Taliban has attacked Christian and Shi'ite targets in their aggressive struggle with the government. A blast in the city of Quetta killed at least 80 people at the Church of Peshawar and injured over 120.[14] In its all-out war, the ruthless tactics of the Taliban are being displayed to show its alignment to the Islamic State. The list of brutal acts of violence continues to grow and continues to illustrate the, "if you aren't with us, then you are against us," mentality being displayed. It is important to point out that the Taliban, just as IS, no longer have regard for borders and are now executing attacks in Pakistan.

The Islamic Movement of Uzbekistan (Afghanistan, Pakistan) This militant group was founded in 1998 by two men, one a former Soviet paratrooper named Juma Namangani, and the other, Islamic ideologue Tahir Yuldashev.[15] The group has recently aligned itself and its ideals very closely to the Taliban and the Islamic State. The Islamic Movement of Uzbekistan (IMU) has moved its base of operations to Afghanistan and is known to cover a large area launching border attacks into Pakistan, Turkmenistan, Uzbekistan, Kyrgyzstan, Iran and Western China.[16] The attacks appear to be intended to discourage, as they are primarily waged against troops from various countries patrolling their borders. It is widely speculated that this militant group protects the areas used as border crossings into neighboring countries for the trafficking of drugs and weapons. This organization is used to recruit members from different regions in Central Asia and maintain control of several strategic borders. It is also believed that this organization is training and sending members into Russia, China and Iran.

Al-Tawhid Battalion (Syria) This organization was created as a result of the Syrian Civil War in an effort to coordinate the battle for Aleppo. In order to create better battlefield efficiency and coordination three rebel units, the Fursan al-jabal Brigade, the Daret Izza Brigade and the Syria Revolutionaries Front joined forces to create the Al-Tawhid Battalion.[17] Initially they criticized IS and refused to be associated with the extreme ways of the Islamic State. However the groups eventually clashed and the leader of Al-Tawhid was captured and tortured to death by IS.[18] Realizing that they could not sustain a two front war they eventually swore allegiance to the Islamic State. This approach has been used very effectively in Syria to help the Islamic State solidify their presence as the dominant Islamic militant group in Syria.

Egyptian Branch of Jund al-Khilafah (Egypt) The name means "Soldiers of the Caliphate" and they have not only sworn allegiance to the Islamic State, but have also vowed to slaughter all Christians in Egypt. In a statement released the leader of the group said "Here are your soldiers fighting those you fight and making peace with those you make peace with."[19] This group has been operating in the Sinai Peninsula since the 2011 revolution against Hosni Mubarak. They are one of a growing number of Islamic militant groups within the Sinai Peninsula swearing allegiance to the Islamic State. It is widely speculated that the group also passes intelligence information to the Islamic State to strike strategic targets, conduct kidnappings, assassinations, and hijack convoys carrying weapons and other supplies.

Alsar-ut Tawhid fi Bilad al-Hind (India) Is an Islamist terrorist group that has been recruiting Muslims in India to fight in Syria and Afghanistan. The group has sworn allegiance to the Islamic State and has expressed its desire to fight against the Hindu majority and establish a caliphate within India.[20,21] This has been the main motivation to establish ties with the Islamic State and to send Muslims to Syria for training and battle hardening.

Ansar Bayt al-Maqdis (Sinai, Egypt) This group has been attacking the Egyptian government, military and police in an effort to create an Islamic State in Egypt and has recently pledged its allegiance to the Islamic State.[22] They have conducted suicide bombings, kidnappings, drive by shootings, and have targeted military units, seizing caches of weapons and ammunition. They recently released a video which showed the beheading of four men accused of working for Israel's Intelligence agency.[23] It is believed that several other militant Islamic terrorist groups have sworn allegiance to the Islamic State and have joined in an effort to disrupt the flow of ships through the Suez Canal. The terror attacks along the canal included naval vessels from the Egyptian fleet. The Suez Canal is a high value target of interest to the Islamic State and we will continue to see operations in that area. IS relentlessly maintains its efforts to defy borders and eliminate passports, and with the ground gained in Syria, it is one step closer to the Suez Canal.

Al Qaeda branch in the Arabian Peninsula (Yemen) The Al Qaeda branch in the Arabian Peninsula (AQAP) is considered one of the deadliest Islamic militant terrorist groups in the world. They are the group responsible for the Charlie Hebdo attack in Paris.[24] The group is believed to be headquartered in Yemen, however the attack in Paris shows it has the ability to reach well beyond its borders. AQAP is considered to be extremely dangerous for several reasons, and it has nothing to do with the amount of weapons or territory it occupies. What makes them both deadly and effective is their recruitment tactics and ability to communicate. The group has a unique ability to contact and communicate with Jihadist globally through the use of an online magazine. The name of the magazine is "Inspire," and the publication is written in English, designed to recruit and communicate with the "would be jihadist" in western countries.[25] Some believe a code is used, hidden within the text of the magazine, to communicate with terrorists. This hidden code is used to launch attacks and communicate with hidden cells. It is also speculated that the AQAP has developed an encryption method that the U.S. agencies and foreign governments can't decipher, allowing them to communicate through email with known terrorists. These are terrifying possibilities that could potentially wreak havoc globally as the world continues to struggle in its endeavor to fight terrorism. These are a few of the reasons why this group is considered so deadly. The recent announcement that they support the Islamic State should come as no surprise and we should be wary of more attacks globally tracing back to the AQAP.

These are some of the most dangerous Islamic terrorist groups in the world and it is easy to see how they have begun to mimic the tactics of the Islamic State. The recent increase in terrorist attacks can be directly attributed to the expansion of the Islamic State. The insidious attacks perpetrated by IS have inspired other organizations to commit even more atrocious acts of violence against humanity. This is where we begin to see the effects of the "cause" that is the Islamic State. We have seen organizations claim allegiance to the black flag of IS bolstering the numbers of the Islamic State, and even adopt the horrific ways of the most extreme Islamic militant terrorist group in the world.

As we continue to examine the effect of the Sunni dominated Islamic State, we must also continue to monitor the Shi'ite responses in various countries. The Shi'ite Muslims understand that the battle will soon be in their cities, streets and neighborhoods. Many have already begun to strengthen their positions within the cities and countries they call home. This has caused many Shi'ite communities to form militias, stockpile weapons and collect ammunition. In numerous places outside of Iraq, Shi'ite Islamic extremists are assisting communities to form resistance groups. Shi'ite extremists' organizations have capitalized on the fear generated by the Islamic State, by organizing the militias and using them to carry out attacks, not only on the Islamic State but also governments and organizations where benefit is seen. These efforts are all in an attempt to solidify their presence within the Middle East. In essence these are the same battles Saladin had to fight before he united Muslims and drove the infidels from the Holy Land.

The effect of this is easily seen in Yemen where the government recently resigned due to pressures from Shi'ite rebels who had the ability to undertake a military style coup. In September of 2014, Shi'ite rebels known as Houthis seized the capitol.[26] With his house and the Presidential palace surrounded, President Abed Rabbo Mansour Hadi announced his resignation through the use of social media, by making the announcement from his official Facebook page in January of 2015.[27] The terrorist militants were trying to pressure him to give a scripted televised speech. Soon after the announcement Prime Minister Khaled Bahah and the entire cabinet submitted resignations.[28] Here we are beginning to see how easily governments are being swayed amidst the chaos in the Middle East.

In the wake of President Hadi's resignation tens of thousands took to the streets to show support for Hadi and denounce the thug tactics of the Houthis militants.[29] Even though Hadi was appointed by a U.N. council and was pro U.S. he provided a stability to the region that had been lacking in recent years and the majority of people responded to his leadership.

The future of Yemen is uncertain, a 33 year ruling regime was toppled in 2011 and the country has struggled to regain footing as terrorist groups have flocked to the region bringing drone strikes and civil unrest with them. The president's resignation created a power vacuum opening the door for jihadi militants to operate. Militant rebels have taken over most of the police stations and have assassinated key government officials in the struggle to maintain the current coup. They have begun shooting protesters who gather to show their discontent with the rebels as Yemen's story continues to unfold amidst turmoil. This is just one more Middle Eastern country in the midst of chaos that is currently or has recently gone through a revolution, civil war or regime change. The entire landscape of the Middle East is changing right before our very eyes, we just have to open them to see it.

FORGING AN EMPIRE

The sky is blue and the desert backdrop captures the lens of the camera as armed men in military fatigues begin marching forward, each escorting a prisoner wearing a blue jumpsuit with hands bound behind their back. As the uniformed fighters march by a container of large knives, the first militant grabs one and the sound effects of an unsheathing sword can be heard as music begins playing. The militants continue to march, each grabbing a knife, the music providing the cadence as they move into position. Only one of the knife wielding fighters is wearing a mask, and upon closer examination of the unmasked militants you can see the faces display a multinational gathering.

Once in position the only masked terrorist, who the British press identifies as "Jihadi John," begins talking. He speaks excellent English coupled with a British accent that grips the words. In a threatening tone he growls in the camera, "To Obama the dog in Rome. Today we slaughter the soldiers of Bashar and tomorrow we will be slaughtering your soldiers and with Allah's permission we break this final and last crusade and the Islamic state will soon, as your puppet David Cameron said, will begin to slaughter your people on your streets." The camera angles begin to change and go in and out of slow motion as they begin showing close-ups of the victims and the terrorist's faces. The masked terrorist, Jihadi John, gives a command and all the victims are forced to their bellies as the extremists place a knee in their backs.

Everyone is now ready with knives placed at the throats of the men awaiting their fate. The first signs of horror grip the victim's faces as the sawing motions commenced and the beheadings began. Blood begins spilling from their necks as the knives saw into flesh. Jihadi John purposely stops half way through making the victim suffer even more while he stares into the camera. With an extra tug Jihadi pulls back on the hair of his victim, allowing the blood to spurt forward into a small trench dug just in front of the men. Another camera zooms in and begins following the trail of blood flowing through the small canal. The blood of the many victims' begins mixing together. The exaggerated sounds of the cutting of flesh can be heard as the chilling scene continues to unfold and one by one the prisoners' heads are removed and placed on top of the decapitated bodies. As the video comes to a conclusion the terrorist stand aside the bloody corpses and a voice speaking in an Arabic language says, "Know that we have armies in Iraq and an army in Sham of hungry lions whose drink is blood and play is carnage."[1]

Closer examination of the video shows production has been enhanced for maximum shock value. Several High Definition cameras providing multiple camera angles were used to capture the killings. The use of sound effects, audio overlays and slow-motion cameras were used to exploit the carnage and emphasize terror. No more backroom grainy single camera productions that made you question if what you were watching was real. It is estimated that the cost of this production was nearly $200,000, and probably took 4-6 hours to complete.[2] The simultaneous beheading of 16 of Bashar's soldiers was a message being sent to the world and no expense was spared. This is the new face of terror being introduced as the world watches in horror. This is the most dangerous militant group the world has ever known, the Islamic State of Iraq and the Levant, better known throughout the world as ISIS, or the Islamic State.

The militants of the Islamic State are marching forth writing the pages of history, while the rest of the world watches in disbelief. The Islamic State is comprised of militant fighters who have shown a willingness to die for their beliefs. Their committed desire to die for those beliefs is what makes them stronger than their adversaries. It is a mindset that believes the closer to death you are the closer to God you are and for this reason they embrace combat. Like moths drawn to a flame we watch the world around us being changed. Mass killings, beheadings, kidnapping, extortion, robbery, organ transplants, nothing is out of bounds and they want the world to know it. Militant extremists have claimed thousands of lives and committed countless acts of terror in their quest to establish the Caliphate that is the Islamic State. They are playing for keeps and all in the name of Islam.

The following is a list of attacks and key incidents in various countries that have attributed to the growth of the Islamic State. These dates reflect battles for military targets, cities, towns, villages, provinces, oil wells, dams and other resources provided by the desert when at war. Also accounted for are the efforts to drive out police and soften Iraqi Defense Forces prior to the large scale offenses. Cities would often undergo days of suicide attacks and car bombings to weaken morale and defenses. The use of these tactics proved to be very successful and showed the combative prowess of the IS leaders in coordinating their efforts.

Once cities were captured IS would use social media to display the mass executions of Iraqi soldiers and police as scare tactics, resulting in a very successful use of media. These horrific media campaigns would cause protecting forces from other cities, towns, and villages to flee prior to or during the onset of attacks. This is one of the reasons why IS was so successful launching a multitude of successive attacks that enabled them to capture a large amount of territory in such a short period of time.

To gaze into the belly of the beast one need only examine the aftermath of the monster's destructive wake. The following information is intended to help illustrate how rapidly events are unfolding. You will find the names, dates, and places of events, coupled with some limited information regarding the occurrences.

Timeline of the Islamic State assaults and events during calendar year 2014

Jan 3rd 2014 – IS seizes control of Fallujah after defeating Iraqi Defense Forces and local police.[3]

Jan 14th 2014 – IS begins a multipronged attack targeting Haditha, Anah, and Rawah. Iraqi Defense Forces withdraw and allow IS to claim Anah and Rawah. The heaviest fighting takes place in Haditha as IS tries to take over the Haditha dam. Through fear that IS will use the dam to flood the city, Iraqi Forces rally and maintain control of the dam.[4]

January 25th 2014 – Several militant groups in Lebanon swear allegiance to IS and announces the creation of the Lebanese extension of IS pledging to fight Hezbollah in Lebanon.[5]

January 30th 2014 – IS militants' fire upon Turkish forces patrolling border. Turkey retaliates with cannon fire, destroying an IS convoy near the border.[6]

February 3rd 2014 – Al Qaeda officially renounces its

ties with ISIS, stating that it had not authorized the presence of ISIS in Syria.[7]

March 8th 2014 – The Prime Minister of Iraq, Nouri al-Maliki, for the first time openly accuses and condemns Saudi Arabia and Qatar of funding and supporting IS.[8]

May 1st 2014 – IS publicly executes seven men in the city of Ar-Raqqah located in northern Syria.[9] The dead are nailed to crosses and displayed as crucifixions. Pictures of the event find their way onto the internet and social media and once again the world is shocked by the brutality of IS.

June 5th 2014 – IS launches attacks in Samarra the city remains contested. The Iraqi Defense Forces claim to have defeated IS; however residents say IS has control of a large portion of the city.

June 7th 2014 – The University of Anbar in Ramadi is overrun by IS militants who capture the University and hold over 1,300 students hostage.[10] Eventually the majority of students are freed after the militants ransack and plunder university resources and materials before being ousted by the Iraqi military.

June 10th 2014 – Once again IS militants use multipronged attacks and lay siege to Mosul, Waleed, Hawija, and Riyad. The IS militants conquer Hawija, Riyad and Mosul rather easily. Mosul, the second largest city in Iraq is now under IS control.[11] This includes the Mosul dam.[12] IS militants also loot the military bases, universities and banks within Mosul while emptying the jails and prisons, allowing the prisoners to join the ranks of IS.[13] Iraqi Defenses pull back and rally to hold on to Waleed because of its strategic value as a border crossing.

June 11th 2014 – With the success of the previous days efforts on June 10th, IS militants continue the push with newly acquired weapons and vehicles and launch attacks on Mishak, Tikrit, Suleiman Bek, Siniyah, Sharqat, Rashad, Karma and continue efforts in Hawija. Mishak, Tikrit and Hawija make a stand and hold out while Suleiman Bek, Siniyah, Sharqat, and Karma fall to the IS. Initially fighters move into Rashad without incident but then clashes break out after IS tries to remove the tribal leaders and people refuse to swear allegiance. IS is driven from Rashad but continues to fight from the outskirts.

June 12th 2014 – After repeated attacks IS gains a foothold in Basheer and Iraqi Shi'ite forces at Camp Speicher, a former U.S. airbase near the city of Tikrit, begin fighting off IS advancements. ISIS captures city of Tikrit.[14]

June 13th 2014 – Saadiyah falls to IS without a fight.[15] Iraqi Defense Forces and Police had abandoned their positions, the cities of Jurf-al Sukhar and Tarmiyah pull together a volunteer defense force and make a stand in an attempt to hold out. Habbaniyah and finally the towns of Qaim, Anah and Rawah fall as IS moves one step closer to Baghdad. IS also claims the assets of the fallen military base in Habbaniyah.[16]

June 14th 2014 – IS captures the city of Dhuluiyah utilizing about 50 weaponized vehicles and encountering little resistance.[17] Several villages in Al Adhaim are overrun by IS militants while attacks in Dujail and Al Khalis are repelled by combined Defense Forces, Police and volunteers.

June 16th 2014 – The Kurdish Peshmerga fighters have begun successfully repelling attacks from IS militants but state that Western support will be required to sustain the efforts.

June 17th 2014 – IS attacks the city of Baquba, Iraqi Defense Forces combine with police and volunteers to repel the attacks.[18] It is also believed that Baquba government officials ordered the execution of prisoners in jail to prevent them from being freed and joining IS. The city of Tal Afar is seized after what was described as brutal fighting with IS militants.[19] The oil fields of Kirkuk are captured by IS.

June 18th 2014 – IS militants attack Al Alam and Khaldiya but were repelled once again by a largely volunteer force. The Ajeel Oil Fields are captured by IS and they begin renewing attacks into Tikrit in an effort to widen areas of control around the captured Oil Fields.[20] It is now speculated that the initial attack on Tikrit days earlier was a feint designed to draw forces away from the neighboring oil fields of Ajeel.

June 19th 2014 – News of attacks on the Baiji Oil Refinery in Albu Bali outside of Baghdad indicate IS has taken control of the facility.[21]

June 21st 2014 – Iraqi forces withdrawal from Al Qai'm in an effort to concentrate efforts to protect Baghdad. IS moves in and immediately assumes control of the strategic border crossing.

June 22nd 2014 – Riding on a wave of confidence stemming from the battle born victories from almost a month of fighting, IS launches attacks against Mahmudiya, Nukhaib, Ruthba, Qayyarah, Trebil, and finally claims victory in Hawija and Waleed capturing

Ash Sharqat and the Qiayara Airbase.[22] The battle for Trebil was thwarted by Jordanian forces that rushed to the border to secure the remote outpost. However Iraqi forces fled the area, allowing IS forces to capture Nukhaib ,Qayyarah and also the city of Mahmudiya, as well as the city of Ruthba which is only located about 90 miles from the Jordanian border. It is evident at this point that the Iraqi Government is feeling overwhelmed and is now allowing other nations to secure its borders in an effort to hold on to Baghdad.

June 23rd 2014 – Trebil is abandoned and taken over by IS. The Anbar Province is now almost completely under IS control.

June 25th 2014 – Once again offenses are launched into multiple locations and the world is beginning to wonder, who is this group called ISIS and what do they want? Two police stations are blown up and a large portion of the city of Ramadi is captured by IS.[23] Balad Airbase is attacked by IS militants but they fail to capture the facility. IS seizes control of the city of Saqlawiyah encountering almost no resistance. Kurdish Pershmerga troops begin resisting attacks in Sinjar while building barriers to repel IS attacks along the southern border. After a series of IED attacks, suicide bombs and days of vicious fighting Tikrit finally falls to IS. The University is plundered and once again jails are emptied to help fill the ranks of IS. After ten days of brutal battle the Baiji Refinery is now completely under IS control.

June 26th 2014 – IS takes control of the border crossing city of Hilliah encountering little resistance. The battle for Camp Speicher continues but eventually falls to IS after heavy fighting.[24] Iraqi troops are captured and then lined up with hands bound behind their back and executed. Images of the horrific mass graves wind up on the internet and social media once again.[25] The initial reports estimate 200-300 troops are killed during the mass execution. A twitter account belonging to an IS member boasts the killing of 1700 Iraqi soldiers.[26] However the graves found later in September would reveal an estimated 800 soldiers were executed during the slaughter[27]. Mansouriyat al Jabal falls and IS assumes control of the Mansuriyah Oil Field.[28]

June 28th 2014 – Rashad finally falls after almost three weeks of fighting. It is rumored that IS has executed the tribal leaders and now has enforced strict sharia law.

June 29th 2014 – This day marks the beginning of the holy month of Ramadan and after a month of vicious fighting throughout the countries of Iraq and Syria Abu Bakr al-Baghdadi announces the establishment of the new Caliphate of the Islamic State and declares himself the Caliph. So after the almost one hundred year absence of a caliphate and caliph, a new leader of the entire Muslim world is declared. The organization officially changes its name from ISIL to IS (Islamic State.)

July 1st 2014 – A convoy of prisoners being transferred from one prison to another in Baghdad is attacked by IS militants. As a result Iraqi forces executed all the prisoners, who were believed to be involved in terrorist activities. Airstrikes target IS militants in and around the city of Mosul as a result of water distribution being cut off to areas north and east of Mosul. Both the city and the dam are still under IS control. Tuz Khurmatu to the north is attacked by IS militants and the Kurds continue to successfully defend their cities and territories.

July 3rd 2014 – IS captures the al-Omar oilfield which is the largest in Syria.[29] The oilfield was under the control of the al-Nusra front and reports indicate that al-Nusra offered no resistance.

July 4th 2014 – Abu Bakr al-Baghdadi makes first public appearance as new self- proclaimed caliph calls on Muslims worldwide to unite and capture Rome as part of an effort to rule the world.

July 9th 2014 – A former chemical weapons facility in al-Awja is captured by IS.[30] There is concern that there may be left over materials, equipment, or instructions that IS can use to manufacture and deploy chemical weapons.

July 11th 2014 – Kurdish Forces move down and take control of two major oil fields on the outskirts of Kirkuk.[31] Previous IS attacks on these targets of interest were repelled and now the largest oil fields in Northern Iraq are under Kurdish control.

July 12th 2014 – A series of suicide bombings occur targeting police stations and security check points in Baghdad.[32] The city goes on high alert in anticipation of a large scale IS assault.

July 14th 2014 – Another large scale assault on Haditha occurs. Iraqi forces are successful in repelling the militant attack and maintain control of both the city and the dam.

July 16th 2014 – Attempts by the Iraqi Defense Forces to retake the city of Tikrit are thwarted by IS troops. Iraqi troops abandon efforts and withdraw from the area leaving the City of Tikrit completely under IS control. IS militants capture and execute 42 Iraqi soldiers in Awenat south of Tikrit.[33]

July 17th 2014 – The northern town of Tuz Khurmatu is captured by IS after significant engagements with the Kurdish Peshmerga fighters. This signifies one of the first defeats suffered by the Kurdish Forces. The Kurds will retake this area; however, the area will become a smuggling route for crude oil being moved onto the black market by IS.[34]

July 17th 2014 – Syria's Shaer gas field located in Homs Governorate is captured by IS militants after a battle that left 270 dead.[35]

July 19th 2014 – IS claims responsibility for an explosion in Baghdad's Kadhimiya district near a Shia shrine which kills 33 and wounds over 50 civilians.[36]

July 22nd 2014 – After having denounced IS, the Sunni Imam Abdul Rahman al-Jobouri was publicly executed in Baquba.[37]

July 24th 2014 – IS militants blow up and destroy the mosque and tomb of the Prophet Yunus or Jonah in Mosul.[38] This is an important holy site not only for Muslims, but also other religions as well.

July 25th 2014 – IS militants capture the Syrian 17th Division Base near Raqqa, beheading captured soldiers and displaying the their heads in the city.[39]

July 26th 2014 – The Shrine of Nabi Shiyt or Prophet Seth is looted and then destroyed.[40] The artifacts taken from the shrine are considered to be priceless.

July 28th 2014 – To mark the end of Ramadan IS releases a 30 minute video which depicts the numerous atrocities committed by the organization, which include mass killings, beheadings, crucifixions and many other heinous crimes against humanity are captured within the video.[41]

August 3rd 2014 – IS militants capture the towns of Sinjar and Zumar. Sinjar was the home of the Yazidi Christian population, an estimated 40,000 Yazidis fled to the mountain regions to escape the wrath of IS. The remaining Yazidi Christians were captured and all the male population was executed in various ways. Thousands of Yazidi girls and women were taken to Tal Afar, Si Basha Khidri and Ba'aj to be sold in slavery.[42] There were many of these young girls and women who were given to IS militants as slaves. The Ain Zalah oil field is also captured by IS with very little resistance.[43]

August 6th 2014 – Bakhdida, Bartella, Hamadaniya, and Tal Kayf are attacked by IS militants.[44] All of these cities have large numbers of Christian inhabitants, including the city of Bakhdida which is also called Qaraqosh, home to the largest population of Christians in Iraq. It is in this area that some of the most heinous crimes against Christian families were committed. Once again many women and young girls captured were sold into slavery or given to IS militants as slaves. Furthermore we again see a religious cleansing take place as many men, women, and children Christians were beheaded or crucified.

August 7th 2014 – Haditha is again attacked by IS militants in an effort to capture the Haditha Dam.[45] The efforts are repelled by Iraqi Defense Forces, however it is evident by the continued attacks that IS considers this a high value strategic target. The town of Makhmour is captured and so is the city of Bashiqa displacing thousands of residents as the number of Iraqi refugees continues to grow.[46]

August 10th 2014 – IS militants attack Tabqa Airbase which is considered to be the last stronghold for the Syrian military in the Raqqah province.[47] The French announce they will consider providing military aid to fight IS militants.[48] IS releases video footage of Yazidi Christians being buried alive. It is estimated around 500 are killed in the video.[49]

August 11th 2014 – In a surprising announcement the UK announces it will not assist the U.S. with airstrikes but will instead increase its humanitarian efforts for the hundreds of thousands displaced in Syria and northern Iraq.[50] The Arab League announces that the atrocities committed by IS are crimes against humanity.[51] IS abducts the commander of the Sahwa Militia in Hawija.[52]

August 13th 2014 – IS captures six villages in Syria near the northern province of Aleppo, close to the Turkish border.[53]

August 15th 2014 – IS learning from the previous attacks on the other Christian dominated cities and witnessing the mass exodus prior to the assaults, surrounded and trapped the Christian inhabitants of the Yazidi village of Kocho so they could not escape. Once trapped the IS militants assaulted the village and killed every male, both young and old totaling over 400 men and boys. Over a 1,000 young girls and women were abducted once again.[54] The images of the attacks on Christians in Northern Iraq captures the world's attention.

August 18th 2014 – Pope Francis announces that it is the international community's responsibility to stop the Islamist militants in Iraq. He also reminded the world that it should not be left up to one nation to decide how to intervene.[55]

August 19th 2014 – American journalist James Foley is beheaded while being videotaped. The release of the video coincides with an announcement from IS claiming that they now have over 50,000 fighters in Syria alone.[56] Iraqi Forces move on the city of Tikrit and engage IS fighters but are halted by heavy resistance.

August 24th 2014 – After nearly two weeks of fighting Tabqa Airbase in Syria is captured.[57] The Sheikh Mand Shrine and the Jidala village shrine were blown up and 14 Yazidi men were killed by IS.[58]

August 26th 2014 – IS claims responsibility for a suicide bomb attack in Baghdad killing 15 and wounding 37 others.[59]

August 27th 2014 – Kurdish forces lay siege to the Ain Zalah oil fields and wrestle control of the fields from IS. The oil fields are set ablaze by IS militants as they retreat.[60]

August 28th 2014 – IS militants release a video showing a Lebanese soldier, Ali al-Sayyed, being beheaded. [61]After clashes near the Lebanese border IS militants capture 19 Lebanese soldiers while briefly occupying a town.

August 29th 2014 – UK Prime Minister David

Cameron announces commitment to fight radical Islam at home and abroad.[62]

August 31st 2014 – German Federal Minister of Defense announced his country will send weapons to Peshmerga fighters in an effort to arm and support those fighting IS.[63]

September 1st 2014 – IS militants set fire to the Yazidi villages of Hareko, Kotan, and Kharag Shafrsky.[64]

September 2nd 2014 – IS releases a video of the beheaded American Journalist Steven Sotloff.[65] In Iraq hundreds of family members of the cadets and soldiers killed at Camp Speicher stormed the Iraqi Parliament demanding explanations regarding the mass killings.[66]

September 4th 2014 – IS issued a threat to President Vladimir Putin, condemning him for his support of al-Assad's regime.[67] IS established Sharia courts begin conducting trials and ordering executions in various cities, towns and villages across Iraq.

September 8th 2014 – The Iraqi Prime Minister Nouri al-Maliki is succeeded by Haider al-Abadi.[68]

September 10th 2014 – In an attempt to discredit and condemn the succession of leaders IS conducts a series of suicide bombings using vehicles in Baghdad that wreak havoc with the Shi'ites.[69]

September 13th 2014 – David Cawthorne Haines, a humanitarian aid worker from the UK was shown beheaded in a video released by IS.[70]

September 21st 2014 – IS militants capture the towns of Saqlawiyah and Sicher. The IS militants also swarm and take control of the Iraqi military base located in Saqlawiyah.[71] Several Iraqi media outlets claim IS militants used chlorine gas during the attack on the Saqlawiyah military base killing 300.[72] Abu Mohammad al-Adnani, a spokeman for IS, releases a statement asking Muslims around the world to kill non-Muslims.[73]

September 22nd 2014 – Iraqi human rights activist Samira Salih al-Nuaimi is publicly executed by IS.[74]

September 24th 2014 – The Algerian terrorist organization Jund al-Khilafah behead the French mountain guide Herve Goudel in retaliation for French participation in the fight against IS.[75]

September 27th 2014 – IS militants clash with Iraqi military patrols in the Albu Aytha area approximately 8 miles south of Baghdad.[76]

September 29th 2014 – A video featuring captive journalist John Camille condemning U.S. President Barrack Obama for U.S. airstrikes is released by IS.[77]

October 2nd 2014 – IS militants detonate several car bombs engaging Iraqi security forces and turn the city of Hit into a battlefield. The Turkish parliament voted successfully to allow anti-IS operations to be conducted from within its borders and to allow Turkish military forces to be sent into Syria to assist in the fight against IS. [78]

October 3rd 2014 – A video released by IS surfaces showing the beheading of British aid worker Alan Henning. The video also threatens captured U.S. aid relief volunteer Peter Kassig.[79]

October 4th 2014 – IS militants continue from Hit and capture Kubaisa.[80] This is a significant event because it cuts off the Ain al-Asad military base which is used to resupply forces defending the Haditha Dam.

October 5th 2014 – A joint effort by al-Nusra and IS invaded Lebanon but are repelled by Hezbollah forces.[81] This is a significant event because the Shi'ite Hezbollah forces engage the Sunni led assaults into Lebanon for the first time.

October 14th 2014 – IS militants capture the city of Hit which forced the Iraqi garrison to abandon the battle after almost two weeks of heavy fighting.[82] A car bomb detonates in Baghdad killing 25 people. One of those killed was a key figure in the Iraqi parliament, Ahmed al-Khafaji.[83,84]

October 16th 2014 – Four car bombs explode in Iraq killing 36 civilians as the efforts to soften Baghdad continue.[85] Italy announces they will send 280 soldiers to train Kurdish fighters.[86]

October 19th 2014 – A suicide bomber attacks a Shia mosque in Baghdad killing 19 and wounding 28.[87]

November 1st 2014 – Multiple car bombings and suicide attacks kill 12 and wound dozens more in Baghdad.[88] The village of Ras al-Maa is overrun by IS militants and 35 villagers and village leaders are buried in a mass grave just outside the village.[89]

November 2nd 2014 – The fighting in Ras al-maa and Haditha continues and it is estimated over 300 of the

Albu Nimr tribe have been killed by IS militants.[90] Multiple car bombings once again targeting Shi'ite Muslims in Baghdad kill 44 and wound 75.[91]

November 3rd 2014 – Leading members from the Islamic State, al-Nusra, Ahrar ash-Sham, the Khorasan Group, and Jund al-Aqsa meet in an attempt to unite and coordinate efforts in Syria.[92] This is a significant occurrence that marks the beginning of an alliance in Syria that will be felt throughout the region.

November 7th 2014 –The U.S. announces it will send 1,500 more troops to Iraq, bringing the total to 3,000 U.S. troops on the ground in Iraq.[93]

November 8th 2014 – A total of 6 car bombings in Ramadi and Baghdad kill 40 and wound 90 more.[94] Car bombings are becoming an almost daily occurrence in Baghdad.

November 16th 2014 – Two videos are released by IS. The first is a video of Peter Kassig whose severed head is shown on the ground. Although the video does not show the actual beheading of Peter Kassig, we are again introduced to Jihadi John as he threatens the U.S. saying Obama lied about withdrawing U.S. forces from Iraq and they wait for the time when they can once again kill American soldiers.[95] The second video is the one featuring the beheading of 16 Syrian soldiers discussed in the beginning of this chapter.[96]

November 23rd 2014 – Iraqi forces team up with Peshmerga fighters and Shi'ite Militia to retake Jalawla which has been under IS control since August.[97] This is a significant occurrence as we see unique forces combining to fight IS militants.

November 25th 2014 – An IS video surfaces on the internet showing two young men being stoned to death by IS militants because it is believed they are homosexual.[98]

December 15-16th 2014 – An armed terrorist named Man Haron Monis entered the Lint Chocolate Café in Sydney Australia and took 10 customers and 8 employees' hostage. Monis had declared his allegiance to Caliph Abu Bakr al-Baghdadi and the Islamic State Caliphate.[99] Several hostages were injured and Monis was shot and killed as the situation climaxed.

December 16th 2014 – India publicly denounces the Islamic State and many fear 39 Indian construction workers held hostage by IS will be executed.[100]

This timeline provided a look at the events in 2014 and based on the acceleration of violence the future is going to be even deadlier. The first few months 2015 has already brought the deadly assault in France. Attacks in which armed Islamic militants stormed a building and executed 12 staff members of the Charlie Hebdo Magazine, claiming revenge for cartoons depicting the Prophet Muhammad.[101] In January IS militants hacked into U.S. military Twitter accounts and threatened U.S. service members participating in attacks against the Islamic State.[102] A video was also tweeted that warned the Islamic State of an upcoming U.S. offensive. These events should make it very clear that we are facing a new kind of enemy that can threaten and wage war in many ways.

Within the first few days of February 2015, a twenty-two minute video of a Jordanian pilot being burned alive was released.[103] The video was so graphic many media outlets refused to show it in its entirety. The twenty-two minute production showed IS militants placing a Jordanian pilot in a small metal cage and then setting him on fire. The camera rolled and they watched as he was burnt alive. The filming never stopped as they dumped trash on the burnt corpse and then crushed the cage with a dozer while his burnt remains were still inside. Towards the end of the video bounties were offered for the successful killing of other Jordanian pilots. Once again the video is utilizing multiple camera angles and indicates a high level of production intended to maximize the horror captured. Videos even went so far as to show pictures, addresses and even Google maps pinpointing the location of the homes of pilots.

Again on February 15th another five minute high quality video using enhanced production would be released. With the ocean's waves cascading onto a beach somewhere in Libya, 21 Coptic Christians from Egypt are shown being beheaded.[104] The lead terrorist wearing brown camouflage and mask is set apart from the rest of the militants who are dressed in black. As the camera settles on the leader he begins to speak, "Safety for you crusaders is something you can only wish for, especially if you are fighting us all together. The sea you have hidden Sheikh Osama Bin Laden's body in, we swear to Allah, we will mix it with your blood."[105] This latest atrocity also marks the largest mass killing performed by the Islamic State outside of Iraq and Syria.

As we examine the evolution of fighting in Iraq, Syria and other areas we continue to see an escalation in the level of violence perpetrated by IS. Bearing witness to this horrific rise in violence it becomes increasingly difficult to understand how politicians in the United States can keep making nonsensical statements when referring to terrorists attacks. Statements that show the world just how unwilling we are to address this problem as a nation. The comment made by former United States Secretary of State, Hillary Clinton, didn't send a very strong message to the global community, when she said we should use "every possible tool and partner leaving no one on the sidelines, showing respect for one's enemies, trying to understand and insofar as psychologically possible, empathize with their perspective and point of view."[106] How do you empathize with people who not only want to kill you, but also rape women and then tell them the only way they can get into heaven is to strap on a suicide vest?

However it is not surprising since it is the same Hillary Clinton who said, "What difference does it make."[107] Those were the callous words she chose when being questioned about the death of our countrymen who were abandoned on foreign soil while honoring their commitment to this once great nation. The fact there has been no response to the attacks that occurred in Benghazi is telling the extremists militants around the globe America is weak and ready for attack.

Yes, the thoughtless comments made by politicians when it comes to war are no longer a surprise, and that in itself is a sad revelation. This is a troubling sign that should warrant the attention of every American as we head into the approaching elections, because we are facing an enemy unlike any we have faced in the past. It is imperative that we have strong leadership as we prepare to engage this new enemy. It would appear a show down with the Islamic State is inevitable, and therefore we must never lose sight of our enemy.

The Islamic State may be in the Middle East, but it has loyal soldiers in almost every country on the planet, including the United States of America. Soldiers who are willing to fight, die, and commit heinous crimes against humanity if but a single word is uttered from the Caliph. No other military on earth can claim that. On March 21st 2015, the Islamic State Hacker Division posted the pictures and information that included the addresses of 100 United States Air Force, Navy and Marine pilots on a website. They also asked for the brothers in America to join the fight and kill these pilots. "Know that it is wajib for you to kill these kuffar! and now we have made it easy for you by giving you addresses, all you need to do is take the final step, so what are you waiting for? Kill them in their own lands, behead them in their own homes, stab them to death as they walk their streets thinking they are safe…"[108] We are witnessing the galvanizing efforts of the most extreme Islamic groups in the world feverishly working to unite the global Muslim community. Do not be mistaken, once they are united the western world will begin to feel the pressure of these Islamic extremists.

SPOILS OF WAR

It seems hard to imagine that an Islamic terrorist group has more weapons and resources than some countries. As of January 2015, the Islamic State was estimated to have over two billion dollars in revenue[1] alone. A wider look at the total assets of the Islamic State by accounting for weapons, vehicles and all other assets of the organization would create a much higher estimate that is difficult to comprehend due to the scale.

As we briefly touched on earlier the Islamic State generates its income much the same way as organized crime members or mobsters do, through the use of strong arm tactics. They have been kidnapping, extorting, robbing and smuggling in efforts to generate revenue to fund their reign of terror. The kidnappings have produced hundreds of millions of dollars in revenue for the organization. It was revealed that IS demanded 132 million dollars from the Global Post for the safe return of James Foley.[2] They have held and released many foreign national hostages after ransoms were paid. However the majority of those, whose ransoms were not met, wound up being beheaded with the gruesome task captured on video for the entire world to see.

They have emptied the banks in every town they have taken over. The Mayor of Mosul reported that the group stole an estimated 400 million in gold bullion and currency.[3] This is only one of the many banks they have emptied during their reign of terror.

The Islamic State controls oil fields and even the Mosul Dam. It is estimated that the oil fields controlled by the Islamic State, although not running at peak efficiency, are generating between two and three million dollars a day.[4] They have kept many of the workers for these oil fields in place, only replacing the upper levels of management. Although a majority of the oil is sold on the black market, it is rumored that they are smuggling the oil out by the use of trucks through Syria and Turkey. The trucks are using forged documents and manifests to make the oil look like it's coming from different areas.

However they are also called the Islamic State and so as a state they have incorporated taxes as a source of revenue. Ledgers used to calculate taxation in certain towns have begun to surface.[5] These ledgers accounting for the levying of tax point to a level of sophistication that we have not seen in previous Islamic militant organizations which mainly operated from the shadows and through donations from supporters. Now we begin to see the gears of the Caliphate of the Islamic State slowly beginning to turn.

The cost of funding the war has required the Islamic State to increase its revenue generating abilities. Fighting a war on multiple fronts has incurred a large debt to sustain fighting capabilities. There is a considerable cost associated with maintaining soldiers in an army; fighters have to be paid something. Some of these costs can be offset by the spoils of war. In what some consider ancient time's men were enticed into battle by promises of the spoils of war. Sometimes land would be bestowed for participation. In many cases share of the plunder would be promised. The Islamic State has in many ways stepped back in time and pays its soldiers in a variety of ways, and in many cases, ways that do not require an exchange of monetary currency. Many of the fighters are paid with slaves taken from the conquered territories.[6] Thousands of women and children have been taken captive never to be seen again. In many prepubescent cases girls have been given to Islamic State militants as slaves.[7] The Islamic State fighters are also being promised land and a position of prominence within the new caliphate to entice their services and fill the ranks. It is estimated that approximately 200 new recruits show up daily to serve and fight in the ranks of the newly formed Caliphate of the Islamic State. These recruits are coming from every corner of the globe, including the United States of America and other western countries.

When we examine the ways in which the Islamic State has established the governing caliphate and has begun to tax the occupants of the state we can see that they are preparing for a long but albeit necessary war to create the new Islamic Empire. The cost of sustaining the established caliphate means IS can't afford to see cash flow diminish on any level. Therefore they are always looking for ways to generate revenue and it deeply influences decisions made by the leaders. Any effort must have a significant payday attached to those efforts, every risk must have reward.

THE THREAT

The threat is real and the Islamic State is waging war on the West and its way of life. In only a few short years the world has watched the Middle East destabilize, one country at a time. As we watched Egypt in the throes of a revolution, Islamist militants attacked Iraq on the heels of the American withdrawal. One by one the cities fell and the world began to hear the chants of ISIS being carried across the desert sands. With each victory their support continued to grow until they erased the border between Iraq and Syria. With each conquest their chants became louder and soon the black flags of the Islamic State can be seen everywhere. Some estimate the numbers to be over 200,000 strong in the Middle East.[1] They use social media in a way the world had yet to experience and shared their triumphs and atrocities, cultivating fear and fervor as blood continued to flow.

Yes they are dangerous and deserve the world's attention as we embark on a new era of war, an era that will test our leaders requiring them to make sound decisions.

A considerable amount of what you are about to read is of my own conclusion. These are my opinions based on personal experience, research and information that I have been exposed to. In this chapter we will examine some strategies and possibilities that lay ahead as we venture into the unknown and try to plot a course for this war that is currently being waged. A war that many believe could lead to the beginning of World War III, Armageddon, or even the coming of the antichrist. Many, including the Islamic State believe biblical revelations are occurring.

In this modern era, fragile economies and aging infrastructures combine to create a volatile atmosphere, which allow countries to be easily destabilized. Destabilization has been the key to success for the Islamic State in its war in the Middle East. Destabilized countries become more vulnerable to attacks and outside influences. The vacuum that was created during the "Arab Spring" has allowed IS to capitalize on the lack of leadership existing in the destabilized countries and regions. It is important to understand that these same factors can affect a world superpower in much the same way. Should an event occur that would destabilize a first world country or superpower, it would have the same crippling effect, making that country extremely vulnerable and considerably less likely to be able to respond to events beyond its own borders.

As we examine some scenarios that could play out and begin the next world war, we must understand that there are certain clandestine possibilities. It is a distinct possibility that the destabilizing attacks may not come from the Islamic State. The attacks could come from another country or group willing to let the blame fall on Islamic extremists. For instance, what if Israel wanted to destabilize Iran? They could use elements of their secret service known as the Mossad to accomplish this. It would be easy to infiltrate Iran and detonate suitcase sized strategic nukes or dirty bombs and allow the blame to be placed on the Islamic State. This type of tactic could be advantageous to Israel as it would then set the Islamic State and Iran against one another.

The attack on Iran could also be seen to have been perpetrated by Israel and that would not be unrealistic. Iran is getting closer to obtaining nuclear weapons and Israel knows that it must do something soon, either with or without the support of the U.S. and the rest of the world. An attack on Iran would most likely prompt retaliation from Iran and also Hezbollah, both would launch attacks into Israel. Iran may choose to use this opportunity to attack Israel regardless of who actually attacked them. Any attack on Israel would almost certainly lead to U.S. intervention, provided the U.S. has the ability to dedicate military resources. This could mark the beginning of the world's descent into World War III

However, in Iran, the borders will be controlled by elements of the Islamic State, which are currently patrolling those borders as mentioned earlier. In the midst of the confusion in Iran the Islamic State could ride in from the west and push the Shi'ite population into the chokeholds of the mountainous borders and begin the persecution as they try to flee. This would be accomplished in much the same way that IS slaughtered the Christian communities of Northern Iraq (Pg.59, 60).

That is one scenario involving Iran and Israel that could trigger a global response, the same could happen in the United States. The reality is Russia, China, Europe or any other country, could also use the disturbance in the Middle East as an opportunity to destabilize the U.S. by detonating weapons of mass destruction within the United States. It is not entirely beyond the realm of reason as the southern border of the U.S. has been used to cross into the United States by more than just South American citizens. Border Patrol agents have reported finding Islamic prayer rugs and other evidence that suggest the borders have been used by Muslims to cross into the United States.[2] We do not know what reason or purpose they would have for infiltrating America, but I am not convinced they have aspirations of a better life. I believe these events signal trouble on the horizon.

Some would say the United States is already on the verge of descending into civil unrest because of racial tensions and a police state that is currently causing palpable strains on the country. Any strike on the U.S. either through the use of a WMD or economic attack, could lead to large scale looting and rioting which would almost certainly enact F.E.M.A. (Federal Emergency Management Agency) and usher in martial law. This would ultimately limit the ability of the U.S. to protect foreign interests and hinder any involvement in a foreign crisis.

The same can be said for parts of Europe and Russia that are currently being contested as civil unrest continues to grow. Europe will undoubtedly have to deal with pressures from the south and east, as well as within its own borders as tensions between Muslims and non-Muslims continue to grow. The recent situation in Ukraine and areas of North Africa are already creating a certain level of destabilization that is currently having a severe effect on our western allies economically. As in the United States, bombs could be detonated in Russia, China and Europe in an attempt to destabilize those countries.

Earlier we examined the smuggling routes into both Russia and China that are controlled by Islamic Militants loyal to the Islamic State (Pg. 42). Any country with enough money could pay these militants to smuggle personnel and WMD's into those countries. The undeniable reality is that these attacks could come from anywhere and be blamed on the Islamic State, not to mention the attacks may very well come from the Islamic State. The point I am trying to illustrate is that the global community is changing rapidly and we may very well be on the brink of another World War. The disappearing lines on maps are indicators of just how volatile the near future is going to be.

It is no secret China is hoarding gold and it is speculated they are waiting for the right opportunity to challenge the dollar in an effort to cripple the U.S. economy.[3] The detonation of nukes or dirty bombs on U.S. soil could trigger that devaluation of the dollar and severely weaken the U.S. on the heels of a cataclysmic event. However China has its own problems and is not immune to the growing threats in the Middle East. If the Islamic State deals a severe blow to Iran and gains control of the oilfields throughout the region, that could potentially create a dire situation ultimately affecting China's oil supply and their ability to govern. Energy shortages occurring on a large enough scale would have devastating consequences on China's manufacturing, production, and distribution capabilities. A certain level of destabilization would occur within the country, which could lead to pressures from outside its borders. This inability to influence foreign affairs could be the strategic timing countries like North Korea are waiting for. These scenarios are not unrealistic; this is the modern world we live in.

It would seem the battle for Iran has already begun; the Islamic State and those who have sworn allegiance to them have in many ways already surrounded the country. The current stance of the Islamic State indicates it will only be a matter of time before they will begin attacking the Shi'ite population of Iran. If you recall some of the information we discussed earlier, Iran is well aware that war is coming for them very soon. It would be safe to assume there are those in Iran who share the belief, that it is only a matter of time before a WMD will be detonated within their borders. Any attack on Iran will surely draw the ire of Russia and China, as they have a vested interest in the oil supplied to them by Iran. The Islamic State has already acknowledged its roll in ushering in Armageddon and they believe it's their duty to set the conditions to allow the coming of their messiah. These types of cataclysmic events could be the sounding of the trumpets and the breaking of the seven seals which will usher in their Armageddon.

A detonation in Iran could be a signal to terrorist cells hidden around the globe. It would stand to reason that soon after the attack on Iran, the Islamic State will detonate dirty bombs, hand held nuclear strikes, or some other weapon of mass destruction, on the West. They will launch attacks into Europe, Russia, the United States and parts of South East Asia. This will destabilize the world's superpowers long enough for attacks to proceed on Iran and Israel. As the superpowers continue to destabilize this would create a window of opportunity for the Islamic State to seize control of the Middle East and expand the state to the size it once was during the height of the Ottoman Empire. This will also allow the new caliphate to control a significant portion of the world's oil supply. At or about the time of the detonations in Iran I believe the Islamic State will be in position to control the Suez Canal and will be able to further dictate the flow of oil from the region. This will increase economic tensions on countries reeling from the atomic detonations and possible economic collapses, thus hindering their ability to intervene in the Middle East. It would appear controlling the oil in the Middle East is the current goal of the Islamic State and the newly established caliphate.

Based on the information gathered during my research, I believe that the majority of the planning was already done by al-Qaeda while Osama Bin Laden was alive. However, Bin Laden's death provided al-Baghdadi with the opportunity to shift control from Ayman al-Zawahiri and take control of the Islamic State. I am convinced that originally he was only to control the Islamic State within Iraq. In my opinion the original plan called for Osama Bin Laden or Ayman al-Zawahiri to be the Caliph of the Islamic State, al-Baghdadi beat him to the punch and declared himself caliph after he was unable to sway al-Jolani in Syria to join him. It would appear that al-Jolani was to represent the leadership of the Islamic State in Syria under the al-Qaeda established caliphate.

The pieces are in place and the Islamic State is waiting for the right time to strike, a time when they are in control of certain strategic locations. As indicated previously, I am convinced Iran plays a pivotal role in the regions end game. Once the avenues allowing Muslims to enter the Islamic State from Europe, Russia, China and Iran are open the trumpets will be sounded, and the world will go to war.

FIGHT TO WIN

In order to fight you must first prepare yourself to fight. The work you do in preparation could be the difference between life and death for you or a family member. Preparation will increase your chances of surviving almost any situation you may find yourself confronted with. Simply put the better prepared you are the higher your chances of survival. The Marine Corps spent a lot of money training me to make sure I was prepared for battle. I was taught how to survive and fight in almost any environment the world has to offer. I am grateful for the training I received because it means I am better prepared to take care of my family in a disastrous situation. I recommend those who read this take a few simple steps to increase your odds of survival in a catastrophic environment.

It is important to store at least 90 days' worth of food, water and life sustaining supplies to use in case you are cut off from other resources. It is also important to be armed with a weapon that you are comfortable operating or using, it makes no sense to have a weapon you are unwilling to use. However, also understand that your ability to comfortably operate multiple weapons systems increases your odds of survival substantially. It is important to be prepared to survive if your house becomes located in a quarantine zone. When nothing is allowed in or out your survival will depend on what you have on hand. The detonation of a dirty bomb or some other WMD could create military enforced quarantine zones. Start collecting at least 90 days' worth of medications and healthcare needs. My suggestion is to eventually have a year's worth of all supplies, however 90 days' worth will substantially increases your odds of survival.

Never forget in your pursuit to investigate and prepare for adversity, knowledge is power. The better informed you are, the more likely to survive you are. Being able to communicate is also an essential part of survival. Make sure you have a short wave or Ham radio in addition to your AM/FM radios. They are available in a wide variety of sizes and capabilities; find the ones that work for you. I also recommend the use of generators to be used in times of power outages. Eliminate debt in your life, do what is necessary to pay off any debt you have accumulated. Doing these things will make you less vulnerable to economic pressure and increase your odds of survival. These are just a few basic tips to hopefully suggest a place to start. Hopefully those who read this book will begin the process to prepare themselves for the dark days ahead.

In the Marine Corps we know only one way to fight, simply stated we "Fight to Win." The world must adopt this same mindset in order to succeed in conquering the Islamic State. This is a war based on ideology that understands no boundaries and will require a herculean effort to thwart their acts of terror. When asked of my opinion I simply state, "This will be a long and hard fought war, but a war we can win." I am certain it will come at a high price because the more desperate the enemy becomes the more desperate their acts will be. If this soulless adversary is cornered I believe they will detonate a weapon of mass destruction on American soil in an effort to test our resolve. It will be up to the American people to show the world that we can withstand the attacks of our enemy and will remain resolute, conquering not only our fears, but also our enemies.

The fight seems to be all around us if we just look close enough, a fact that must be realized in order to defeat the Islamic State. Presently there is a war of ideals being fought around the world. Western law and way of life are being challenged by radical Islamic movements. This is what makes engaging this enemy particularly challenging, we are fighting an ideal that can be manifested anywhere in the world. There are many who believe an agenda has been adopted that is slowly transforming western countries into Islamic States. Countries around the globe are being inundated with Muslim refugees from the fighting in the Middle East. Populations within Muslim communities in western cities are dramatically increasing in size.

When Muslim extremists are attacking police officers with hatchets on the streets of New York, there is a problem.[1] When a Muslim goes on a rampage and shoots innocent people like what happened in Fort Hood, we should not allow it to be referred to as a case of "workplace violence." When a woman is beheaded by a Muslim coworker in Oklahoma we shouldn't let it be described as "workplace violence."[2] It is important to recognize these dreadful acts of violence for what they are, "acts of terrorism," perpetrated by radical Islamic extremists on behalf of their religious beliefs. We see innocent people being tortured and slaughtered, and then we are asked to sympathize and empathize with our enemies. We watch as the enemy posts wanted pictures on the internet asking Muslims in America to kill our nation's heroes. Now is not the time to allow the government to be coy when it is our future that is in peril.

It is the responsibility of the entire world to let elected officials know that acts of terror, perpetrated by radicalized Islamist extremists, will not be tolerated. This effort will require a global opposition to the application of Sharia law. Stepping back into the dark ages is unacceptable, nor will we recognize or tolerate a country that wishes to do so. This effort will require an unwavering commitment to maintaining our standards and principles. It is vital that western countries, cities and communities, do not change because of pressure from the Muslim communities.

It is time for the world to unite and stand against these indecent crimes against the innocent. It is important that we do not empathize with any country or organization that is involved with genocide or religious persecution. We must be vigilant in the way we honor the men and woman who fight for our countries and stand up for our freedoms. The message must be conveyed, that it is unacceptable to allow an Imam to give the opening prayer on national television to open the congressional session during a week that celebrates our nations heroes, Veterans Week.[3] I know there were enough American born military veteran heroes willing to say the prayer. Everyone should defend our nation's heroes and not let any administration deprive them of the medical and social needs they require. It is important that we let our government know that we will not tolerate the deep cuts to retirement and medical benefits for our military veterans. It is important to stand strong and let our nation's leaders know that these things are not acceptable. The current administration has failed to properly represent the American people and the United States is being portrayed as a weakening nation ready to be assaulted. The proof of this is in the attacks on the embassy in Benghazi. As stated earlier the United States lack of response to that incident was perceived as a greenlight for jihadist organizations around the globe. Since the attack on Benghazi the number of terror attacks around the globe has skyrocketed. This is not coincidence; this is a direct result of our political posturing in regards to the Middle East.

The war against the Islamic State begins with the

American people taking a stand. We must again show the world that we are not weak, and the time has come to end the religious and ethnic cleansing taking place in the Middle East. We must prepare for war because war is being prepared for us. These are defining moments, not only in our nation's history but that of the world. Times that require situations to be handled a particular way. Now more than ever we cannot afford to appear weak in front of our enemy. If it is truly our goal to defeat the Islamic State then it is important that the United States of America be recognized as a guiding force in the world. If we want to win then it is our duty to see to the destruction of the Islamic State. Sometimes things must be that simple.

Multinational assaults on multiple fronts will be needed to destroy the Islamic State. Their failures will be measured by our successes; victories must be won both on and off the battlefield. To counter the growth of Islamic State it will require the identification of IS leaders to be targeted for termination. In addition we will need to recognize and target their revenue streams in an effort to interrupt and take away their ability to generate cash flow. If the goal is to defeat the Islamic State, than now is not the time for a politically correct approach. The lack of respect they have for humanity dictates the credence of our enemy. They must not be underestimated, to do so would be a dire mistake.

Unfortunately these goals will likely not be realized without U.S. forces being deployed to the Middle East again. We will have to once again depend on our allies to support this effort to combat global terrorism. However, our strength will reside in our resolve and we should be willing to do what is necessary in order to stop these terrorist militants from spreading fear. That will be the stern type of leadership needed to defeat the Islamic State.

The struggle to fight the Islamic extremists must not be that of the United States alone. There are local Middle Eastern groups willing to help in this fight. Groups such as the "Sons of Iraq," have stated their desire to work with the U.S.[4] There have been several leaders who have pledged man power to bring an end to the Islamic State. The Kurdish people of Northern Iraq have had sustained success fighting the Islamic State. Although they are willing to fight they have made it very clear they lack the resources to sustain a prolonged engagement. It is important that these local resources be cultivated to assist in the efforts. In some cases as many as 10,000 men have been assembled by these organizations. They lack the resources and training and have asked the U.S. for assistance to help arm and train the men. The hope in suppressing the threat can be found in the willingness of men and women who are ready to fight the Islamic State.

However there are many in Washington who are opposed to using these resources and in some cases rightly so. It would not be beyond the realm of possibility that we would be training and arming the enemy once again. There is little doubt of the precarious circumstances in the Middle East, however I think given the horrific nature of the Islamic State some chances will have to be taken. There are several organizations that have received a stamp of approval from the CIA and been deemed worthy of receiving training and supplies.

Time is of the essence in this war to halt the growth of the Islamic State. There are many who agree sending American forces back to the Middle East is inevitable, which means that it should be done sooner as opposed to later. Some estimates say that a force of at least 50,000 troops would be necessary to eliminate IS control just in Iraq alone.[5] As IS continues gaining ground and claiming territory, the numbers required to break their hold will only continue to grow. This continued growth will only make the efforts more difficult as they rally troops and accumulate more resources, resources that could have detrimental if not deadly consequences. Every day they are one step closer to building weapons of mass destruction.

At a time when our nation is once again pressed with a need for military action our current administration has announced that the U.S. will be making severe cuts to the military. This decision is not a reflection of what is in the best interest of our nation. Downsizing our military will only make the decision to go back the Middle East that much more difficult when the time comes. However after the jaw dropping deficit incurred by the recent administration we are hardly left with any other choice. The fact that we continue to bolster the size of homeland defense at the expense of our military is cause for concern. It has been speculated that the implementation and growth of Homeland Security is a response to a perceived need to handle the continuing civil unrest that continues to grow within the United States. This can in some ways be seen as a resignation to the troubles in the Middle East, it may very well be that we are readying for the inevitable use of WMDs on American soil.

The detonation of a WMD in America should be a matter of great concern to everyone. The repercussions of an event such as that would be felt throughout the world in every land. One would be justified in expressing concern over whether or not the U.S. Government, in its current state, will act in the best interest of the people. There is never a shortage of wolves ready to capitalize on the weak when fear and confusion are in the air. In the words of Winston Churchill and Rahm Emanuel "Never let a good crisis go to waste."

A nuclear, biological, or chemical, attack occurring within the United States would certainly trigger a state of emergency. This could result in FEMA being enacted and martial law being instituted. This would effectively abolish our government in its current form and induce a police state. Under these circumstances one could perceive the need for more homeland defense and less military power. There are plenty who would interpret these events as calculated efforts to undermine the United States constitution and strip Americans of the rights bestowed upon them by this once great nation. If this is indeed the case, then one would fear we may have already lost not only the war but also our way of life. Only time will tell.

My time in the Marine Corps taught me that American men and women are capable of extraordinary things. I have witnessed Americans perform incredible acts of bravery and heroism. This enemy we are facing is not invulnerable, we are stronger than them and they can be beaten. It is time for Americans to once again stand tall and join together in an effort to make this nation and the world a safer place to live, grow, and prosper. The blessings of this great nation and wonderful world are deserving of those who are willing to pursue liberty and justice for all.

"At its greatest hour of need a once great nation thirsts for the stout leadership it has known for 238 years. Unfortunately we have our own madrassas, we call them universities. They produce drones incapable of rational thought, other than that spoon fed to them by the pajama boys and girls who matriculated from Ivy League schools, whose major concerns are global warming, reproductive rights and redistributing the wealth of those who work for a living. Should I make the cut and get to go to heaven, I'm not sure I would be capable of looking our Founding Fathers in the face. How could we let this happen to our republic?"

The Colonel

Notes

CHAPTER ONE: JIHAD

1. New Cambridge History of Islam Vol. 3
   Cambridge Histories Online © Cambridge
   University Press, 201 1
   http://archive.org/stream/TheNewCambridgeHis
   toryOfIslamVolume1/The_New_Cambridge_Hist
   ory_of_Islam_Volume_3_djvu.txt
2. History Staff, "Saladin" 2012,
   http://www.history.com/topics/saladin
3. Kennedy Hickman, "Crusades: Siege of Jerusalem"
   http://militaryhistory.about.com/od/battleswars10
   011200/p/jerusalem.htm
4. "CIA's Operation Cyclone in Afghanistan," Russia
   Today, The U.S. made Soviet Trap, Feb 15th 2009,
   https://www.youtube.com/redirect?q=http%3A%
   2F%2Fwww.russiatoday.com%2Ffeatures%2Fnew
   s%2F37327&redir_token=Oq6DpZyYmpM21lUid
   iVodZzKyW18MTQyNTQ0MzEzMkAxNDI1Mz

U2NzMy

5. Mr. Weiser & Ms. Sachs "U.S. Sees Brooklyn Link to World Terror Network" The New York Times Oct 22nd 1998, http://www.nytimes.com/1998/10/22/world/us-sees-brooklyn-link-to-world-terror-network.html

6. Ahmad Rashid, Taliban, New Haven: Yale University Press, 2002, p. 130.

7. Andrew Gavin Marshall, "The Imperial Anatomy of Al-Qaeda. The CIA's Drug-Running Terrorists and the "Arc of Crisis," Global Research," Sept 4th 2010, http://www.globalresearch.ca/the-imperial-anatomy-of-al-qaeda-the-cia-s-drug-running-terrorists-and-the-arc-of-crisis/20907

8. Wright, Lawrence, "The Rebellion Within," Jun 2nd 2008, The New Yorker. 84 (16). pp. 36–53

9. Bruce Riedel, "The 9/11 Attacks' Spiritual Father," Sept 11th 2011, The Daily Beast. http://www.thedailybeast.com/articles/2011/09/11/abdullah-azzam-spiritual-father-of-9-11-attacks-ideas-live-on.htmlPut source reference here

10. Steven Emerson, "Osama Bin Laden's Special Operations Man," Sept 1st 1998, Journal of Counterterrorism and Security International. http://www.investigativeproject.org/187/osama-bin-ladens-special-operations-man#

11. Lawrence Wright, "The Looming Tower: Al-Qaeda and the Road to 9/11," 2006, pp.195

12. Lawrence Wright, "The Looming Tower: Al-Qaeda and the Road to 9/11," 2006, pp.186

13. David Horowitz, "How the Left Undermined America's Security before 9/11," March 24th 2004, FrontPageMag.com http://archive.frontpagemag.com/readArticle.aspx?ARTID=13676

14. Dan Edge, "Children of the Taliban," 2009, October Films Production WGBH/Frontline.

15. Phil Ponce "Admiral William Crowe," Jan 8th 1999, PBS News Hour

16. Maria Rasmussen and Mohammed Hafez, "Terrorist innovations in weapons of mass effect: preconditions, causes, and predictive indicators," Oct 2010, Calhoun, USN. http://hdl.handle.net/10945/25358

17. "How much did the September 11 terrorist attack cost America?" 2004, Institute for the Analysis of Global Security. http://www.iags.org/costof911.htm

18. BBC Archive, "Transcript: Bin Laden video excerpts," Dec 27th 2001, BBC News. http://news.bbc.co.uk/2/hi/middle_east/1729882.stm

19. CNN Library, "Operation Enduring Freedom Fast Facts," Dec 31st 2014, CNN News. http://www.cnn.com/2013/10/28/world/operation-enduring-freedom-fast-facts/index.html

CHAPTER TWO: BORN OF CHAOS

1. Larry Diamond, "What Went Wrong in Iraq" October 2004, Foreign Affairs. <http://www.foreignaffairs.com/articles/60095/larry-diamond/what-went-wrong-in-iraq>.

2. History.com Staff, "Saddam Hussein Captured" 2010, History Channel, http://www.history.com/this-day-in-history/saddam-hussein-captured

3. History.com Staff, "Saddam Hussein Captured" History Channel, 2010, http://www.history.com/this-day-in-history/saddam-hussein-captured

4. History.com Staff, "Saddam Hussein Captured" History Channel, 2010, http://www.history.com/this-day-in-

history/saddam-hussein-captured

5. "Confrontation in the Gulf; Excerpts From Iraqi Document on Meeting With U.S. Envoy," Sept 23rd 1990, New York Times. http://www.nytimes.com/1990/09/23/world/confrontation-in-the-gulf-excerpts-from-iraqi-document-on-meeting-with-us-envoy.html?pagewanted=7&src=pm/

6. The Baghdad Pact; Origins and Political Setting, 1956, Royal Institute of Internal Affairs. http://www.worldcat.org/title/baghdad-pact-origins-and-political-setting/oclc/23997916

7. "Abd al-Karim Qasim," Encyclopædia Britannica. Encyclopædia Britannica Online. Encyclopædia Britannica Inc., 2015 http://www.britannica.com/EBchecked/topic/485552/Abd-al-Karim-Qasim

8. Abbas Ali, "Saddam: Washington's Faithful Dictator," Jan 8th 2007, World Security Network. http://www.worldsecuritynetwork.com/Iraq/abbas-ali-1/Saddam-Washington's-Faithful-Dictator

9. CNN Library, "Saddam Hussein Fast Facts," Oct 17th 2013, CNN News. http://www.cnn.com/2013/10/17/world/meast/saddam-hussein-fast-facts/

10. Octavia Nasr, "Tape: Bin Laden tells Sunnis to fight shiites in Iraq," Jul 2nd 2006, CNN.com. http://www.cnn.com/2006/WORLD/meast/07/02/binladen.message/

11. James Dorsey, "Islamic State Urges FIFA to Deprive Qatar of the World Cup," Jul 9th 2014, The World Post/ Huffington Post. http://www.huffingtonpost.com/james-dorsey/islamic-state-urges-fifa_b_5569524.html

12. Nicholas Schmidle, "Getting Bin Laden: What happened that night in Abbottabad," Aug 8th 2011, The New Yorker.

http://www.newyorker.com/magazine/2011/08/08/getting-bin-laden

13. Bruce Riedel, "Is Anwar al-Awlaki Osama Bin Laden's Successor?" May 5th 2011, Newsweek. http://www.newsweek.com/anwar-al-awlaki-osama-bin-ladens-successor-67679

14. Primoz Manfreda, "Definition of the Arab Spring" 2011, About News/About.com. http://middleeast.about.com/od/humanrightsdemocracy/a/Definition-Of-The-Arab-Spring.htm

15. Michael Slackman, "Egyptian Emergency Law is Extended for 2 Years," May 11th 2010, The New York Times. http://www.nytimes.com/2010/05/12/world/middleeast/12egypt.html?_r=0

16. Ernesto Londono and Greg Miller, "CIA Begins Weapons Delivery to Syria." Sept 11th 2013, The Washington Post. http://www.washingtonpost.com/world/national-security/cia-begins-weapons-delivery-to-syrian-rebels/2013/09/11/9fcf2ed8-1b0c-11e3-a628-7e6dde8f889d_story.html

17. Tim Lidster, "ISIS: The first terror group to build an Islamic state?" Jun 12th 2014, CNN. http://www.cnn.com/2014/06/12/world/meast/who-is-the-isis/

18. Jamie Dettmer, "Syria's Al Qaeda Gang Wars" Jan 1st 2009, The Daily Beast. http://www.thedailybeast.com/articles/2014/01/09/syria-s-al-qaeda-gang-wars-between-jabhat-al-nusra-and-isis.html

19. BBC Library, "Profile: Abu Bakr al-baghdadi," Jul 5th 2014, BBC News, BBC Middle East. http://www.bbc.com/news/world-middle-east-27801676

20. Liz Sly, Al-Qaeda disavows any ties with radical Islamist ISIS group in Syria, Iraq" Feb 3rd 2014,

The Washington Post.
http://www.washingtonpost.com/world/middle
_east/al-qaeda-disavows-any-ties-with-radical-
islamist-isis-group-in-syria-
iraq/2014/02/03/2c9afc3a-8cef-11e3-98ab-
fe5228217bd1_story.html

21. Souad Mekhennet, "The terrorist fighting us
    now? We just finished training them," Aug 18th
    2014, The Washington Post.
    http://www.washingtonpost.com/posteverythin
    g/wp/2014/08/18/the-terrorists-fighting-us-
    now-we-just-finished-training-them/

22. Taylor Wofford, "ISIL, ISIS or IS? The
    Etymology of the Islamic State," Sept 16th 2014,
    Newsweek.
    http://www.newsweek.com/etymology-islamic-
    state-270752

23. Philip Ewing, "General: ISIL battle in Iraq could
    take 3 years or more," Dec 18th 2014,
    POLITICO.
    http://www.politico.com/story/2014/12/isil-us-
    iraq-timeline-of-fighting-113679.html

CHAPTER THREE: THE MAN IN BLACK

1. Patrick Goodenough, "Self-Appointed 'Caliph'
   Makes First Public Appearance" Jul 6th 2014,
   cnsnews.com.
   http://cnsnews.com/news/article/patrick-
   goodenough/self-appointed-caliph-makes-first-
   public-appearance

2. BBC Library, "Profile: Abu Bakr al-baghdadi,"
   Jul 5th 2014, BBC News, BBC Middle East.
   http://www.bbc.com/news/world-middle-east-
   27801676

3. Janine Giovonni, "Whos is ISIS Leader Abu Bakr
   al-Baghdadi?" Dec 8th 2014, Newsweek.

http://www.newsweek.com/2014/12/19/who-isis-leader-abu-bakr-al-baghdadi-290081.html

4. Janine Giovonni, "Whos is ISIS Leader Abu Bakr al-Baghdadi?" Dec 8th 2014, Newsweek. http://www.newsweek.com/2014/12/19/who-isis-leader-abu-bakr-al-baghdadi-290081.html

5. Janine Giovonni, "Whos is ISIS Leader Abu Bakr al-Baghdadi?" Dec 8th 2014, Newsweek. http://www.newsweek.com/2014/12/19/who-isis-leader-abu-bakr-al-baghdadi-290081.html

6. Terrance McCoy, "How ISIS leader Abu Bakr al-Baghdadi became the world's most powerful jihadist leader," Jun 11th 2014, http://www.washingtonpost.com/news/morning-mix/wp/2014/06/11/how-isis-leader-abu-bakr-al-baghdadi-became-the-worlds-most-powerful-jihadi-leader/

7. Michael Daly, "ISIS Leader: 'See you in New York," Jun 14 2014, The Daily Beast. http://www.thedailybeast.com/articles/2014/06/14/isis-leader-see-you-in-new-york.html

8. Bill Roggio, "US and Iraqi forces kill Al Masri and Baghdadi, al Qaeda in Iraq's top two leaders" Apr 19th 2010, The Long War Journal. http://www.longwarjournal.org/archives/2010/04/al_qaeda_in_iraqs_to.php

9. Mark Hosenball, "Has the Leader of Al Qaeda in Iraq Been Captured?" May 4th 2009, Newsweek. http://www.newsweek.com/has-leader-al-qaeda-iraq-been-captured-79815

CHAPTER FOUR: CALIPHATE

1. Alessandria Masi, "Where To Find ISIS Supporters: A Map Of Militant Groups Aligned With The Islamic State Group," Oct 9th 2014, International Business Times.

http://www.ibtimes.com/where-find-isis-supporters-map-militant-groups-aligned-islamic-state-group-1701878

2. Alessandria Masi, "Where To Find ISIS Supporters: A Map Of Militant Groups Aligned With The Islamic State Group," Oct 9th 2014, International Business Times. http://www.ibtimes.com/where-find-isis-supporters-map-militant-groups-aligned-islamic-state-group-1701878

3. "Umayyad dynasty," Encyclopædia Britannica. Encyclopædia Britannica Online. Encyclopædia Britannica Inc., 2015. Accessed Feb 22nd 2015, http://www.britannica.com/EBchecked/topic/6 13719/Umayyad-dynasty

4. "Abu Bakr," Faithology, Faithology LLC. 2015. Accessed Feb 23rd 2015, http://www.faithology.com/biographies/abubak

5. "Umayyad dynasty," Encyclopædia Britannica. Encyclopædia Britannica Online. Encyclopædia Britannica Inc., 2015. Accessed Feb 22nd 2015, http://www.britannica.com/EBchecked/topic/6 13719/Umayyad-dynasty

6. BBC Library, "Sunnis and Shia in the Middle East," Dec 19th 2013, BBC News, BBC Middle East. http://www.bbc.com/news/world-middle-east-25434060

7. BBC Library, "Sunnis and Shia in the Middle East," Dec 19th 2013, BBC News, BBC Middle East. http://www.bbc.com/news/world-middle-east-25434060

8. Sandra Johnson, "How Did Islam Grow?" People, Opposing Views, Demand Media. http://people.opposingviews.com/did-islam-grow-6046.html

9. Alim Library, "Khalifa Abu Bakr – Successor to the Holy Prophet," Dec 18th 2014, Alim.com. http://www.alim.org/library/biography/khalifa/content/KAB/7/4

10. Tim Lidster, "What does Iran get for supporting al-Assad?" Aug 13th 2012, CNN News. http://www.cnn.com/2012/08/08/world/syria-iran-analysis/index.html

11. David D. Kirkpatrick & Rukmini Callimachi, "Islamic State Video Shows Beheadings of Christians in Libya," Feb 15th 2015, The New York Times. http://www.nytimes.com/2015/02/16/world/middleeast/islamic-state-video-beheadings-of-21-egyptian-christians.html?_r=0

12. Tim Arango, "Maliki Agrees to Relinquish Power in Iraq," Aug 14th 2014, The New York Times. http://www.nytimes.com/2014/08/15/world/middleeast/iraq-prime-minister-.html

13. "The Sunni Shia Divide," 2015, Council on Foreign Relations. http://www.cfr.org/peace-conflict-and-human-rights/sunni-shia-divide/p33176#!/

14. "Iran-Iraq War (1980-1988)" Nov 7th 2011, GlobalSecurity.org http://www.globalsecurity.org/military/world/war/iran-iraq.htm

15. Helene Cooper & Mark Landler, "U.S. Officials Say Iran Has Agreed to Nuclear Talks," Oct 20th 2012, The New York Times. http://www.nytimes.com/2012/10/21/world/iran-said-ready-to-talk-to-us-about-nuclear-program.html?pagewanted=all

CHAPTER FIVE: CAUSE AND EFFECT

1. Jeremy Bender, "ISIS Has Seized Iraq's Largest

Dam, And What Happens Next Is Crucial," Aug 7th 2014, Business Insider. http://www.businessinsider.com/isis-has-seized-the-mosul-dam-2014-8

2. Noah Rayman, "Iraq Militants Seize Old Chemical Weapons Facility," Jun 19th 2014, Time. http://time.com/2901562/iraq-isis-chemical-weapons/

3. "ISIL Seizes Egypt Navy boat in 'most daring terrorist attack in decades,'" Dec 4th 2014, World Tribune, WorldTribune.com. http://www.worldtribune.com/2014/12/04/isil-seizes-egypt-navy-boat-daring-terrorist-attack-decades/

4. Perry Chiaramonte, "ISIS seizes uranium from lab; experts downplay 'dirty bomb' threat," Jul 10th 2014, Fox News, FoxNews.com. http://www.foxnews.com/world/2014/07/10/isis-seized-uranium-compounds-from-lab-experts-downplay-threat/

5. Ibrahim Abdulaziz & Haruna Umar, "Amnesty: Nigeria Massacre Deadliest In History Of Boko Haram" Jan 9th 2015, The World Post, The Huffington Post. http://www.huffingtonpost.com/2015/01/09/amnesty-nigeria-massacre-boko-haram_n_6444680.html

6. Robyn Dixon, "Leader of Boko Haram says God told him to carry out massacre," Jan 21st 2015, The LA Times. http://www.latimes.com/world/africa/la-fg-nigeria-boko-haram-massacre-20150121-story.html

7. Dr. Sebastian Gorka, "Orwell and the Administration: The White House as the Ministry of Truth," Feb 3rd 2015, The Counter Jihad Report. http://counterjihadreport.com/tag/abu-

bakr-al-baghdadi/

8. "Algerian Islamic militants behead French hostage," Sept 25th 2014, The Eagle-Tribune. http://www.eagletribune.com/news/algerian-islamic-militants-behead-french-hostage/article_9577965e-c101-5b44-8c29-377a1ed3a6e8.html

9. Faisal Irshaid, "Profile: Libya's Ansar al-Sharia," Jun 13th 2014, BBC News. http://www.bbc.com/news/world-africa-27732589

10. Jon Mitchell, "War In Libya and Its Futures: State of – Islamist Forces," Jan 26th 2015, The Red (Team) Analysis Society. https://www.redanalysis.org/tag/islamic-state/

11. Sharron Ward, "The Battle of the Shrines," Sept 9th 2014, Foreign Policy. http://foreignpolicy.com/2012/09/12/the-battle-of-the-shrines/

12. Ulysses Arn, "Emptying Gitmo: Obama Trades 5 Terrorists for 1 POW: House Passes Spending for Gitmo North," Jun 1st 2014, Red State. http://www.redstate.com/diary/ulyssesarn/2014/06/01/emptying-gitmo-obama-trades-5-terrorist-1-pow-house-passes-spending-gitmo-north/

13. Sophia Saifi & Greg Botelho, "In Pakistan school attack, Taliban terrorists kill 145, mostly children," Dec 17th 2014, CNN News. http://www.cnn.com/2014/12/16/world/asia/pakistan-peshawar-school-attack/index.html

14. "Pakistan Blasts: Burials amid anger after Peshawar church attack," Sept 23rd 2014, BBC News. http://www.bbc.com/news/world-asia-24201240

15. "Islamic Movement of Uzbekistan," Mar 15th 2015, Australian National Security, Australian

National Security website.
http://www.nationalsecurity.gov.au/Listedterrori
storganisations/Pages/IslamicMovementofUzbe
kistan.aspx

16. "Islamic Movement of Uzbekistan," Mar 15th
2015, Australian National Security, Australian
National Security website.
http://www.nationalsecurity.gov.au/Listedterrori
storganisations/Pages/IslamicMovementofUzbe
kistan.aspx

17. Jeffrey Bolling, "Rebel Groups in Northern
Aleppo Province," Aug 29th 2014, Institute for
the Study of War. UnderstandingWar.org
http://www.understandingwar.org/sites/default/
files/Backgrounder_RebelGroupsNorthernAlepp
o.pdf

18. "ISIS Attacks Rebel Base in Aleppo," Feb 1st
2014, Syrian National Coalition Of Syrian
Revolution and Opposition Forces.
http://www.etilaf.org/en/press/isis-attacks-
rebel-base-in-aleppo.html

19. Gianluca Mezzofiore, "Egypt: Isis- linked Jund
Al-khilafah Threatens to Kill Christians," Sept
30th 2014, International Business Times.
http://www.ibtimes.co.uk/egypt-isis-linked-jund-
al-khilafah-threatens-kill-christians-1467862

20. "Ansar-ut Tawhid fi Bilad al Hind (aut)"
Terrorism Research & Analysis Consortium,
TRAC.
http://www.trackingterrorism.org/group/ansar-
ut-tawhid-fi-bilad-al-hind-aut%20

21. Raj Shekhar, "ISIS-linked terror group Ansar-ut
Tawhid fi Bilad al Hind vows to avenge Batla
House encounter," Sept 20th 2014, The
Economic Times, India.
http://articles.economictimes.indiatimes.com/20
14-09-20/news/54135464_1_batla-house-indian-

mujahideen-encounter

22. "Egypt court begins trial for over 200 alleged
    Ansar Bayt al-Maqdis members," Mar 5th 2015,
    Aswat Masriya.
    http://en.aswatmasriya.com/news/view.aspx?id
    =2e6641b9-482c-469a-a3ab-c18617fa64ee

23. Umberto Bacchi, "Egyptian Jihadists Behead
    'Mossad Spies" in Gruesome Video," Aug 28th
    2014, International Business Time.
    http://www.ibtimes.co.uk/egyptian-jihadists-
    behead-mossad-spies-gruesome-video-1463024

24. Catherine E. Shoichet & Josh Levs, "Al Qaeda
    branch claims Charlie Hebdo attack was years in
    the making," Jan 21st 2015, CNN News.
    http://www.cnn.com/2015/01/14/europe/charl
    ie-hebdo-france-attacks/index.html

25. Stephen Rex Brown, "Vietnamese man charged
    with joining Al Qaeda in Yemen extradited to
    New York," Mar 3rd 2015, New York Daily
    News. http://www.nydailynews.com/new-
    york/nyc-crime/man-charged-joining-al-qaeda-
    yemen-extradited-nyc-article-1.2135980

26. Matt Roberts, "Yemen Rebels Seize Military Base
    Outside Capitol," Jan 29th 2015, ATW News,
    Around the World News Network.
    http://atwnetwork.com/2015/01/29/yemen-
    rebels-seize-military-base-outside-capital/

27. Abdelhak Mamoun, "Urgent: Yemeni President
    Abed Rabbo Mansour Hadi resigns," Jan 23rd
    2015, Iraqi News.
    http://www.iraqinews.com/arab-world-
    news/urgent-yemeni-president-abed-rabbo-
    mansour-hadi-resigns/

28. Abdelhak Mamoun, "Urgent: Yemeni President
    Abed Rabbo Mansour Hadi resigns," Jan 23rd
    2015, Iraqi News.
    http://www.iraqinews.com/arab-world-

news/urgent-yemeni-president-abed-rabbo-mansour-hadi-resigns/

29. "Thousands rally against Shiite militia in Yemen Capitol," Jan 24th 2015, The Jordan Times. http://jordantimes.com/thousands-rally-against-shiite-militia-in-yemen-capital

CHAPTER SIX: FORGING AN EMPIRE

1. Dawn Perlmutter, "Latest IS Beheading Video: New Levels of Ritual Madness," Nov 17th 2014, Tulisan Murtad. http://tulisanmurtad.blogspot.com/2014/11/latest-is-beheading-video-new-levels-of.html

2. Naina Bajekal, "ISIS Beheading Video Took 6 Hours to Film and Multiple Takes," Dec 9th 2014, Time Magazine, Time Inc. Network. http://time.com/3624976/isis-beheading-technology-video-trac-quilliam/

3. Laura Smith-Spark & Ashley Fantz, "Obama: Iraq needs U.S.,international help as ISIS threatens to seize more cities," Jun 13th 2014, CNN News. http://www.cnn.com/2014/06/12/world/meast/iraq-violence/index.html

4. "Iraqi City in Hands of Al-Qaida-Linked Militants," Jan 4th 2014, Voice of America. http://www.voanews.com/content/iraqi-city-in-hands-of-alqaidalinked-militants/1823591.html

5. "Al-Qaeda-linked groups expand into Lebanon," Jan 26th 2014, Al Jazeera. http://www.aljazeera.com/news/middleeast/2014/01/al-qaeda-group-says-lebanese-shia-are-targets-201412643312606443.html

6. Scott Lucas, "Syria: Turkey Hits Islamic State of Iraq Convoy Near Border," Jan 29th 2014, EA World View.

http://eaworldview.com/2014/01/syria-turkey-hits-islamic-state-iraq-convoy-near-border/

7. Oliver Holmes, "Al Qaeda breaks link with Syrian militant group ISIL," Feb 3rd 2014, Reuters. http://www.reuters.com/article/2014/02/03/us-syria-crisis-qaeda-idUSBREA120NS20140203

8. Ned Parker & Louise Ireland, "Iraqi PM says Saudi, Qatar openly funding violence in Anbar," Mar 9th 2014, Reuters. http://www.reuters.com/article/2014/03/09/us-iraq-saudi-qatar-idUSBREA2806S20140309

9. Salma Abdelaziz, "Death and desecration in Syria: Jihadist group 'crucifies' bodies to send message," May 2nd 2014, CNN News. http://edition.cnn.com/2014/05/01/world/meast/syria-bodies-crucifixions/index.html?hpt=hp_c1

10. Ghazwan Hassan, "Iraq dislodges insurgents from city of Samarra with airstrikes," Jun 5th 2014, Reuters. http://www.reuters.com/article/2014/06/05/us-iraq-security-idUSKBN0EG1RG20140605

11. Liz Sly & Ahned Ramadan, "Insurgents seize Iraqi city of Mosul as security forces flee," Jun 10th 2014, The Washington Post. http://www.washingtonpost.com/world/insurgents-seize-iraqi-city-of-mosul-as-troops-flee/2014/06/10/21061e87-8fcd-4ed3-bc94-0e309af0a674_story.html

12. Alissa J. Rubin & Rod Nordland, "Sunni Militants Advance Toward Large Iraqi dam," Jun 25th 2014, The New York Times. http://www.nytimes.com/2014/06/26/world/middleeast/isis-iraq.html

13. Liz Sly & Ahned Ramadan, "Insurgents seize Iraqi city of Mosul as security forces flee" Jun

10th 2014, The Washington Post.
http://www.washingtonpost.com/world/insurge
nts-seize-iraqi-city-of-mosul-as-troops-
flee/2014/06/10/21061e87-8fcd-4ed3-bc94-
0e309af0a674_story.html

14. "Iraq city of Tikrit falls to ISIL fighters –
Gunmen from the Islamic State of Iraq take city
and launch attacks on Kirkuk and Samarra, a day
after the fall of Mosul," Jun 12th 2014, Al Jazeera.
http://www.aljazeera.com/news/middleeast/201
4/06/iraqi-city-tikrit-falls-isil-fighters-
2014611135333576799.html

15. Simon Tomlinson, "ISIS jihadists now seize
Saadiyah and Jalawla en route to Baghdad using
U.S. military vehicles and weapons stolen from
fleeing western-trained Iraqi forces," Jun 13th
2014, Capitol Bay.
http://www.capitalbay.com/latest-
news1/526383-isis-jihadists-now-seize-saadiyah-
and-jalawla-en-route-to-baghdad-using-u-s-
military-vehicles-and-weapons-stolen-from-
fleeing-western-trained-iraqi-forces.html

16. "Iraqi Sunni insurgents seize huge cache of US-
made arms and equipment," Jun 13th 2014,
News.com.
http://www.news.com.au/world/iraqi-sunni-
insurgents-seize-huge-cache-of-usmade-arms-
and-equipment/story-fndir2ev-1226952811362

17. Bill Roggio, "Analysis: ISIS, Allies Reviving
'Baghdad Belts' Battle Plan" Jun 14th 2014,
Foundation for Defense of Democracies.
http://defenddemocracy.org/media-hit/bill-
roggio-analysis-isis-allies-reviving-baghdad-belts-
battle-plan/

18. Tova Dvorin, "ISIS Attacks Baquba on
Approach to Baghdad," Jun 17th 2014, Arutz
Sheva, Israelnationalnews.com.

http://www.israelnationalnews.com/News/New
s.aspx/181826#.VPk5nJstHIU

19. Tova Dvorin, "ISIS Attacks Baquba on Approach to Baghdad," Jun 17th 2014, Arutz Sheva, Israelnationalnews.com. http://www.israelnationalnews.com/News/New s.aspx/181826#.VPk5nJstHIU

20. "Sunni militants reportedly take control of small oil fields, attack air base in Iraq," June 25th 2014, Fox News. http://www.foxnews.com/world/2014/06/25/ir aq-pm-concentrates-troops-around-baghdad-as-iraq-becomes-increasingly/

21. Islamists seize most of main Iraqi oil refinery at Baiji," June 18th 2014, France 24. http://www.france24.com/en/20140618-isis-islamists-attack-iraq-oil-refinery-baiji/

22. "Iraq Updates," Jun 21st 2014, Institute for the Study of War. http://iswiraq.blogspot.com/

23. "Isis militants capture three towns in Iraq's Anbar," Jun 22nd 2014, The Irish Times. http://www.irishtimes.com/news/world/middle -east/isis-militants-capture-three-towns-in-iraq-s-anbar-1.1841366

24. Bill Roggio, "Islamic State storms Camp Speicher, routs Iraqi forces," Jul 19th 2014, The Long War Journal. http://www.longwarjournal.org/archives/2014/ 07/islamic_state_overru.php

25. Bill Roggio, "Islamic State storms Camp Speicher, routs Iraqi forces," Jul 19th 2014, The Long War Journal. http://www.longwarjournal.org/archives/2014/ 07/islamic_state_overru.php

26. Bill Roggio, "Islamic State storms Camp Speicher, routs Iraqi forces," Jul 19th 2014, The Long War Journal.

http://www.longwarjournal.org/archives/2014/
07/islamic_state_overru.php

27. Bill Roggio, "Islamic State storms Camp
    Speicher, routs Iraqi forces," Jul 19th 2014, The
    Long War Journal.
    http://www.longwarjournal.org/archives/2014/
    07/islamic_state_overru.php

28. Bill Roggio, "ISIS advances on oil fields in
    Salahaddin, Diyala," Jun 26th 2014, Threat Matrix,
    The Long War Journal.
    http://www.longwarjournal.org/threat-
    matrix/archives/2014/06/isis_advances_on_oil_
    fields_in.php

29. Sylvia Westall, "ISIS seizes oil field and towns in
    Syria's east," Jul 3rd 2014, Al Arabia News.
    http://english.alarabiya.net/en/News/middle-
    east/2014/07/03/ISIS-seizes-oil-field-and-
    towns-in-Syria-s-east.html

30. "ISIS seizes former chemical weapons plant in
    Iraq," Jul 9th 2014, The Guardian.
    http://www.theguardian.com/world/2014/jul/0
    9/isis-seizes-chemical-weapons-plant-muthanna-
    iraq

31. Nabih Bulos, "Iraq tension increases as Kurdish
    forces seize oil fields," Jul 11th 2014, LA Times.
    http://www.latimes.com/world/middleeast/la-
    fg-iraq-kurdish-forces-oil-20140711-story.html

32. "Insurgents Attack Town North of Baghdad" Jul
    13th 2014, Reuters, The Chicago Tribune.
    http://articles.chicagotribune.com/keyword/bag
    hdad

33. "Report on the Protection of Civilians in Armed
    Conflict in Iraq: 6 July – 10 September 2014,"
    Oct 10th 2014, Human Rights Office of the High
    Commissioner for Human Rights.
    https://web.archive.org/web/20141009043028/
    http://www.ohchr.org/Documents/Countries/I

Q/UNAMI_OHCHR_POC_Report_FINAL_6J
uly_10September2014.pdfKk

34. Mohammed Hussein, Christine Van Den Toorn, Patrick Osgood and Ben Lando, "ISIS earning $1M per day from Iraqi oil smuggling," Iraqi Economist Network.
http://iraqieconomists.net/en/2014/07/13/isis-earning-1m-per-day-from-iraqi-oil-smuggling-by-by-mohammed-hussein-christine-van-den-toorn-patrick-osgood-and-ben-lando/

35. "Hundreds Killed' in Syrian gas field capture," Jul 19th 2014, Aljazeera.
http://www.aljazeera.com/news/middleeast/2014/07/islamic-state-fighters-seize-syria-gas-field-2014717134148345789.html

36. "Islamic State says carried out Baghdad suicide bombing," Jul 23rd 2014, Rueters.
http://www.reuters.com/article/2014/07/23/us-iraq-security-idUSKBN0FS0QZ20140723

37. Hawar Berwani, "Clergyman killed in eastern Baquba," Jul 22nd 2014, Iraqi News.
http://www.iraqinews.com/iraq-war/clergyman-killed-in-eastern-baquba/

38. "Iraq jihadists blow up 'Jonah's tomb' in Mosul," Jul 25th 2014, Agence France-Presse, The Telegraph.
http://www.telegraph.co.uk/news/worldnews/middleeast/iraq/10989959/Iraq-jihadists-blow-up-Jonahs-tomb-in-Mosul.html

39. Johnlee Varghese, "ISIS Captures Syrian Military Base in Raqqa, Beheads Soldiers," Jul 25th 2014, International Business Times.
http://www.ibtimes.co.in/isis-captures-syrian-military-base-raqqa-beheads-captured-soldiers-605356

40. Staff Writer, "ISIS destroys prophet Sheth shrine in Mosul," Jul 26th 2014, Al Arabiya News.

http://english.alarabiya.net/en/News/middle-east/2014/07/26/ISIS-destroy-Prophet-Sheth-shrine-in-Mosul-.htmlAAA

41. Damien McElroy, "Islamic State jihadists issue 30-minute killing spree on video," The Telegraph.
http://www.telegraph.co.uk/news/worldnews/middleeast/syria/11000079/Islamic-State-jihadists-issue-30-minute-killing-spree-on-video.html

42. "Report on the Protection of Civilians in Armed Conflict in Iraq: 6 July – 10 September 2014," Oct 10th 2014, Human Rights Office of the High Commissioner for Human Rights.
https://web.archive.org/web/20141009043028/http://www.ohchr.org/Documents/Countries/IQ/UNAMI_OHCHR_POC_Report_FINAL_6July_10September2014.pdfKk

43. ISIS's latest oil field gains not to hurt KRG's exports according to expert," Aug 3rd, 2014, Daily Sabah.
http://www.dailysabah.com/economy/2014/08/03/isiss-latest-oil-field-gains-not-to-hurt-krgs-exports-according-to-expert

44. "Christians flee as jihadists attack northern Iraq," Aug 6th 2014, The Daily Star.
http://www.dailystar.com.lb/News/Middle-East/2014/Aug-06/266239-christians-flee-as-jihadists-attacks-northern-iraq.ashx

45. Hamza Mustafa, "Haditha Dam under threat from ISIS, warns official," Aug 19th 2014, Asharq Al-Awsat.
http://www.aawsat.net/2014/08/article55335627/haditha-dam-under-threat-from-isis-warns-official

46. Patrick Cockburn, "Isis: Iraqi army retakes control of oil refinery as Kurds stand firm against

overstretched Islamic State," Nov 14th 2014, The Independent.
http://www.independent.co.uk/news/world/middle-east/isis-the-kurds-strike-back--army-retakes-control-of-oil-refinery-town-as-kurds-stand-firm-against-overstretched-isis-9862538.html

47. Muhammad Iqbal, "Syrian troops defending last stronghold in Raqa province," Aug 21st 2014, Business Recorder.
http://www.brecorder.com/top-news/1-front-top-news/189593-syrian-troops-defending-last-stronghold-in-raqa-province.html

48. "France to consider arming Iraqi Kurds battling ISIS," Aug 11th 2014, France 24.
http://www.france24.com/en/20140810-france-consider-arming-iraq-kurds-battling-isis-fabius/

49. Ahmed Rasheed, "Iraq Says ISIS Killed 500 Yazidis And Buried Some Victims Alive," Aug 10th 2014, business Insider.
http://www.businessinsider.com/r-exclusive-iraq-says-islamic-state-killed-500-yazidis-buried-some-victims-alive-2014-10

50. Thomas Penny, "U.K. Ruled Out Iraq Air Strikes as Increased Aid Planned," Aug 11th 2014, Bloomberg Business.
http://www.bloomberg.com/news/articles/2014-08-11/u-k-rules-out-iraq-air-strikes-as-increased-aid-planned

51. Staff Writer, "Arab League denounces ISIS attacks as 'crimes against humanity," Aug 11th 2014, Al Arabiya New.
http://english.alarabiya.net/en/News/middle-east/2014/08/11/U-S-weighs-options-to-evacuate-trapped-Yazidis-.html

52. "Report on the Protection of Civilians in Armed Conflict in Iraq: 6 July – 10 September 2014,"

Oct 10th 2014, Human Rights Office of the High Commissioner for Human Rights. https://web.archive.org/web/20141009043028/ http://www.ohchr.org/Documents/Countries/I Q/UNAMI_OHCHR_POC_Report_FINAL_6J uly_10September2014.pdfKk

53. "Islamic State advances in Syria's Aleppo province: NGO," Aug 13th 2014, Agence France-Presse. http://www.afp.com/en/node/2722462

54. "Report on the Protection of Civilians in Armed Conflict in Iraq: 6 July – 10 September 2014," Oct 10th 2014, Human Rights Office of the High Commissioner for Human Rights. https://web.archive.org/web/20141009043028/ http://www.ohchr.org/Documents/Countries/I Q/UNAMI_OHCHR_POC_Report_FINAL_6J uly_10September2014.pdfKk

55. R. Milhem & H. Said "The Vatican denounces ISIS crimes, calls for wide condemnation," Aug 13th 2014, SANA: Syrian Arab News Agency. http://www.sana.sy/en/?p=9970?1804ea90?ce1c 36a0

56. "American journalist James Foley beheaded by ISIS," Aug 19th 2014, CNN. http://pix11.com/2014/08/19/us-probes-claim-american-journalist-james-foley-beheaded-by-isis/

57. "ISIS captures major air base in Syria," Aug 24th 2014, CBS News. http://www.cbsnews.com/news/isis-captures-major-air-base-in-syria/ AAA

58. "Report on the Protection of Civilians in Armed Conflict in Iraq: 6 July – 10 September 2014," Oct 10th 2014, Human Rights Office of the High Commissioner for Human Rights. https://web.archive.org/web/20141009043028/ http://www.ohchr.org/Documents/Countries/I

Q/UNAMI_OHCHR_POC_Report_FINAL_6J
uly_10September2014.pdfKk

59. "Car bomb kills 15 at busy Baghdad intersection," Aug 26th 2014, The Daily Star, Lebanon.
http://www.dailystar.com.lb/News/Middle-East/2014/Aug-26/268520-car-bomb-kills-10-at-busy-baghdad-intersection-officials.ashx

60. "Militants burn three Iraq oil wells as Iraq;s Kurds attack," Aug 28th 2014, Al Arabiya News.
http://english.alarabiya.net/en/News/middle-east/2014/08/28/Militants-burn-three-Iraq-oil-wells-as-Iraq-s-Kurds-attack-.html

61. Mariam Karouny, Robin Pomeroy, Leslie Adler, "Islamic State militants behead captive Lebanese soldier: video," Aug 30th 2014, Reuters.
http://www.reuters.com/article/2014/08/30/us-syria-crisis-beheading-idUSKBN0GU0J020140830

62. David Cameron, "Threat level from international terrorism raised: PM Press Statement," Aug 29th 2014, GOV.UK.
https://www.gov.uk/government/speeches/threat-level-from-international-terrorism-raised-pm-press-conference

63. Sabine Siebold, "Germany to send Iraqi Kurds enough weapons for 4,000 fighters," Aug 31st 2014, Reuters.
http://www.reuters.com/article/2014/08/31/us-iraq-security-germany-idUSKBN0GV0TY20140831

64. "Report on the Protection of Civilians in Armed Conflict in Iraq: 6 July – 10 September 2014," Oct 10th 2014, Human Rights Office of the High Commissioner for Human Rights.
https://web.archive.org/web/20141009043028/http://www.ohchr.org/Documents/Countries/I

Q/UNAMI_OHCHR_POC_Report_FINAL_6J
uly_10September2014.pdfKk

65. Jack Mirkinson, "Steven Sotloff, American Journalist, Beheaded by ISIS," Sept 2nd 2014, The Huffington Post. http://www.huffingtonpost.com/2014/09/02/st even-sotloff-beheaded-isis_n_5753564.html

66. markomalley, "Relatives of Slain Soldiers Storm Parliament Building in Baghdad," Sept 2nd 2014, Free Republic. http://www.freerepublic.com/tag/news-forum/index?more=3199533

67. "Islamic State says Vladimir Putin's throne is 'under threat and will fall when we come to you'" Sept 4th 2014, http://www.smh.com.au/world/islamic-state-says-vladimir-putins-throne-is-under-threat-and-will-fall-when-we-come-to-you-20140903-10c4hq.html

68. Loveday Morris and Liz Sly, "Iran endorses Haider al-Abadi as Iraq's new Prime Minister, spurning Nouri al- Maliki," Aug 12th 2014, The Washington Post. http://www.washingtonpost.com/world/middle _east/iran-endorses-haider-al-abadi-as-iraqs-new-prime-minister-spurning-nouri-al-maliki/2014/08/12/0487f02c-222c-11e4-8593-da634b334390_story.html

69. Sameer N. Yacoub, "Attacks kill 30 people in Iraq's capitol, Baghdad," Sept 10th 2014, Yahoo News. http://news.yahoo.com/double-car-bomb-attack-kills-10-iraq-112731744.html

70. Rukmini Callimachi and Kimiko De Freytas-Tamura, "ISIS Video Shows Execution of David Cawthorne Haines, British Aid Worker," Sept 13th 2014, The New York Times http://www.nytimes.com/2014/09/14/world/m

iddleeast/islamic-state-says-it-has-executed-david-cawthorne-haines-british-aid-worker.html?_r=0

71. Abdelhak Mamoun, "URGENT: ISIS kills 300 Iraqi soldiers by chlorine gas attack in Saqlawiyah," Sept 22nd 2014, Iraqi News. http://www.iraqinews.com/iraq-war/urgent-isis-kills-300-iraqi-soldiers-chlorine-gas-attack-saqlawiyah/

72. Abdelhak Mamoun, "URGENT: ISIS kills 300 Iraqi soldiers by chlorine gas attack in Saqlawiyah," Sept 22nd 2014, Iraqi News. http://www.iraqinews.com/iraq-war/urgent-isis-kills-300-iraqi-soldiers-chlorine-gas-attack-saqlawiyah/

73. Robert Spencer, "Islamic State Spokesman: Rely upon Allah, and kill, American, European, Austrailian, and Canadian non-Muslims," Sept 22nd 2014, Jihad Watch. http://www.jihadwatch.org/2014/09/islamic-state-spokesman-rely-upon-allah-and-kill-american-european-australian-and-canadian-non-muslims

74. NBC's Baghdad Produce and Christina Boyle, "Leading Iraqi human Rights Activist Killed After Anti-ISIS Posts," Sept 25th 2014, NBC News. http://www.nbcnews.com/storyline/isis-terror/leading-iraqi-human-rights-activist-killed-after-anti-isis-posts-n211441

75. "IS-linked terror group Jund al-Khilafah behead French hostage Herve Gourdel, who was kidnapped in Algeria on Sunday," Sept 25th 2014, News.com. http://www.news.com.au/world/islinked-terror-group-jund-alkhilafah-behead-french-hostage-herve-gourdel-who-was-kidnapped-in-algeria-on-sunday/story-fndir2ev-1227069708096

76. NBC News Staff, "ISIS Seizes Weapons After Overruning Iraq's Albu Aytha Base," Oct 1st 2014, NBC News. http://www.nbcnews.com/storyline/isis-terror/isis-seizes-weapons-after-overrunning-iraqs-albu-aytha-base-n215586

77. "John Cantlie: Third video of UK hostage released," Sept 29th 2014, CNN News. http://www.bbc.com/news/uk-29420897 AAA

78. Laura Smith-Spark, Chelsea J. Carter and Gul Tuysuz, "Turkish lawmakers OK military action against ISIS," Oct 2nd 2014, CNN News. http://www.cnn.com/2014/10/02/world/meast/isis-air-strikes/

79. Chelsey J. Carter, Mariano Castillo and Selma Abdelaziz, "ISIS video claims to show beheading of Alan Henning; American threatened," Oct 3rd 2014, CNN News. http://www.cnn.com/2014/10/03/world/meast/isis-alan-henning-beheading/index.html?hpt=hp_t1

80. "Town Falls to Islamic State in Iraq's Angbar Province," Oct 4th 2014, Reuters, News Week. http://www.newsweek.com/town-falls-islamic-state-iraqs-anbar-province-275366 AAA

81. Nidal Al-Solh, "Calm returns to border after Hezbollah-Nusra fighting killed 22," Oct 6th 2014, The Daily Star, Lebanon. http://www.dailystar.com.lb/News/Lebanon-News/2014/Oct-06/273047-five-hezbollah-fighters-dead-in-border-clashes.ashx

82. "Islamic State militants overrun the strategic city of Heet and claim half Syrian border town of Kobane," Oct 14th 2014, News.com. http://www.news.com.au/world/islamic-state-militants-overrun-the-strategic-city-of-heet-and-claim-half-syrian-border-town-of-kobane/story-

fndir2ev-1227089645199

83. Vivian Salama & Sameer N. Yacoub, "Militants take Iraq army camp as bombs hit Baghdad," Oct 14th 2014, The Boston Globe. http://www.bostonglobe.com/news/world/201 4/10/13/militants-take-iraq-army-camp-bombs-hit-baghdad/HLYAekQR7Y62Ekevpjy9cN/story.html

84. Ahmed Hussein, "Parliament mourns late Khafaji," Oct 15th 2014, Iraqi News. http://www.iraqinews.com/baghdad-politics/parliament-mourns-late-khafaji/

85. "36 Killed in IS Attacks on Baghdad's Shi'ite Areas," Oct 16th 2014, Reuters, Voice of America. http://www.voanews.com/content/islamic-state-attacks-baghdad-car-bombs-mortar-rounds/2485931.html

86. Ria Novosti, "Italy to Send 280 Soldiers to Train Kurds Fighting Islamic State: Defense Minister" Oct 17th 2014, Global Security.org. http://www.globalsecurity.org/wmd/library/ne ws/iraq/2014/iraq-141017-rianovosti01.htm

87. "Deal agreed for Australian forces to deploy in Iraq, Foreign Minister Julie Bishop says," Oct 19th 2014, Reuters, ABC News. http://www.abc.net.au/news/2014-10-20/iraq/5825438

88. "Baghdad area bombings kill at least 24," Nov 2nd 2014, AAP, Sky News. http://www.skynews.com.au/news/world/mide ast/2014/11/02/baghdad-area-bombings-kill-at-least-24.html

89. "Death toll from ISIS' public executions of Iraqi Sunni tribesmen passes 200," Nov 3rd 2014, CBS News. http://www.cbsnews.com/news/death-

toll-from-isis-public-executions-of-iraqi-sunni-tribesmen-passes-200/

90. Michael Georgy, "ISIS Militants Kill Over 300 Members Of Defiant Iraqi Tribe," Nov 2nd 2014, The World Post, The Huffington Post. http://www.huffingtonpost.com/2014/11/02/isis-albu-nimr-massacre_n_6089678.html

91. "Car bombs in Baghdad kill 44, injure 75," Nov 2nd 2014, Middle Ease Eye. http://www.middleeasteye.net/news/islamic-state-militants-carry-out-mass-killings-iraqi-tribe-2103321319

92. Deb Riechmann, "AP Sources: IS, al-Qaida reach accord in Syria," Nov 13th 2014, Yahoo News. http://news.yahoo.com/ap-sources-al-qaida-reach-accord-syria-190921017.html

93. CNN Library, "U.S. to Send More Troops to Iraq; President Obama Set to Pick New Attorney General; President Meets With Republicans," Nov 7th 2014, CNN Transcript, CNN News. http://transcripts.cnn.com/TRANSCRIPTS/1411/07/cnr.07.html

94. "Fresh Iraq blasts kill at least 31 in Baghdad," Nov 8th 2014, Al Arabiya. http://english.alarabiya.net/en/News/middle-east/2014/11/08/Car-bombs-kill-12-in-Baghdad-Ramadi.html

95. Catherine Herridge, "New ISIS video shows beheading of American hostage Peter Kassig," Nov 16th 2014, Fox News. http://www.foxnews.com/world/2014/11/16/new-isis-video-purportedly-shows-beheading-american-hostage-peter-kassig/

96. Amir Abdallah, "URGENT Video: Peter Kassig beaded by ISIS with 16 Syrians," Nov 16th 2014, Iraqi News. http://www.iraqinews.com/features/urgent-

video-peter-kassig-beheaded-isis-16-syrians/

97. Saif Hameed, "Iraqi forces say retake two towns from Islamic State," Nov 23rd 2014, Reuters. http://www.reuters.com/article/2014/11/23/us -mideast-crisis-iraq-towns- idUSKCN0J70AX20141123

98. "NGO: ISIS stones 2 gay men to death is Syria," Nov 25th 2014, News 24. http://www.news24.com/World/News/NGO- ISIS-stones-2-gay-men-to-death-in-Syria- 20141125

99. Alastair Jamieson, Cassandra Vinograd, M. Alex Johnson and Miranda Leitsinger, "Sydney Siege Ends: Police Storm Cafe Where Man Haron Monis Held Hostages," Dec 15th 2014, NBC News. http://www.nbcnews.com/storyline/sydney- hostage-standoff/sydney-siege-ends-police- storm-cafe-where-man-haron-monis-n268321

100. "India bans ISIS, hunts for sympathisers," Dec 16th 2014, The Indian Express. http://indianexpress.com/article/india/india- others/india-bans-isis-hunts-for-sympathisers/

101. "Charlie Hebdo: Al-Qaeda in Yemen claims it ordered attack in line with Osama bin Laden's 'warnings," Jan 9th 2015, The Independent. http://www.independent.co.uk/news/world/eur ope/charlie-hebdo-alqaeda-in-yemen-claims-it- ordered-attack-in-revenge-for-mohamed- cartoons-9969366.html

102. Dan Friedman, Sasha Goldstein & Ginger Adams Otis, "U.S. Central Command Twitter account hacked by ISIS cyber group as White House admits mistake over Paris march," Jan 12th 2014, Daily News New York. http://www.nydailynews.com/news/national/u- s-central-command-twitter-account-hacked-isis-

article-1.2074848

103. "ISIS Burns Jordanian Fighter Pilot Alive," Feb 4th 2015, Democracy Now. http://www.democracynow.org/2015/2/4/head lines

104. David D. Kirkpatrick & Rukmini Callimachi, "Islamic State Video Shows Beheadings of Egyptian Christians in Libya," Feb 15th 2014, The New York Times. http://www.nytimes.com/2015/02/16/world/m iddleeast/islamic-state-video-beheadings-of-21-egyptian-christians.html?_r=0

105. David D. Kirkpatrick & Rukmini Callimachi, "Islamic State Video Shows Beheadings of Egyptian Christians in Libya," Feb 15th 2014, The New York Times. http://www.nytimes.com/2015/02/16/world/m iddleeast/islamic-state-video-beheadings-of-21-egyptian-christians.html?_r=0

106. "Clinton says America should 'empathize' with its enemies," Dec 5th 2014, Fox News. http://www.foxnews.com/politics/2014/12/05/ clinton-says-america-should-empathize-with-its-enemies/

107. Jim Treacher, "What difference does it make whether Hillary Clinton lied about Benghazi?," May 6th 2014, The Daily Caller. http://dailycaller.com/2013/05/06/what-difference-does-it-make-whether-hillary-clinton-lied-about-benghazi/

108. Jason Molinet, "ISIS hackers call for homegrown 'jihad' against U.S. military, posts names and addresses of 100 service members," Mar 21st 2015, New York Daily News. http://www.nydailynews.com/news/national/isi s-hackers-call-jihad-u-s-military-article-1.2157749

CHAPTER SEVEN: SPOILS OF WAR

1. Sarah Spickernell, "Islamic State's $2bn budget is much smaller than those of the countries it is trying to take over," Jan 6th 2015, City AM. http://www.cityam.com/206532/why-islamic-states-2bn-budget-nothing-worry-about-face-its-enemies

2. Andrew Hart, "ISIS Email To Family Of Executed American Journalist James Foley Revealed," Aug 21 2014, Huffington Post, The World Post. http://www.huffingtonpost.com/2014/08/21/isis-email-james-foley_n_5698530.html

3. Jack Moore, "Mosul Seized: Jihadis Loot $429m from City's Central Bank to Make Isis World's Richest Terror Force," Jun 11th 2014, International Business Times. http://www.ibtimes.co.uk/mosul-seized-jihadis-loot-429m-citys-central-bank-make-isis-worlds-richest-terror-force-1452190

4. Chis Dalby, OilPrice.com, "Who Is Buying The Islamic State's Illegal Oil?" Oct 1st 2014, Peak Oil. http://peakoil.com/consumption/who-is-buying-the-islamic-states-illegal-oil

5. Howard J. Shatz, "To Defeat the Islamic State, Follow the Money," Sept 10th 2014, Rand Corporation. http://www.rand.org/blog/2014/09/to-defeat-the-islamic-state-follow-the-money.html

6. Donna Rachel Edmunds, "ISIS Jihadists Forcing Yazidi Women to Work as Sex Slaves," Sept 13th 2014, Breitbart. http://www.breitbart.com/london/2014/09/13/jihadists-using-women-to-run-brothels/

7. Faith Karimi & Greg Botelho, "ISIS putting price tags on Iraqi children, selling them as slaves, U.N.

says," Feb 6th 2015, CNN News.
http://www.cnn.com/2015/02/06/world/isis-children-torture/

CHAPTER EIGHT: THE THREAT

1. Patrick Cockburn, "War with Isis: Islamic militants have army of 200,000, claims senior Kurdish leader," Nov 16th 2014, The Independent.
    http://www.independent.co.uk/news/world/middle-east/war-with-isis-islamic-militants-have-army-of-200000-claims-kurdish-leader-9863418.html

2. Sara Carter, "The Odd Book One Texas Rancher Found Near the Border here," Jul 14th 2014, The Blaze.
    http://www.theblaze.com/stories/2014/07/14/urdu-dictionary-found-on-texas-ranch-near-border-we-just-dont-know-whos-here-already/

3. Eric McWhinnie, "China hoarding gold to challenge U.S. dollar?" Nov 9th 2014, USA Today.
    http://www.usatoday.com/story/money/markets/2014/11/09/cheat-sheet-china-gold/18644197/

CHAPTER NINE: FIGHT TO WIN

1. "Hatchet-Wielding Man Shot Dead in New York After Police Officer Critically Wounded," Oct 24th 2014, Reuters, Newsweek.
    http://www.newsweek.com/new-york-police-officer-critically-wounded-hatchet-attack-279567

2. Greg Botelho, "Police: FBI probing past of suspect in Oklahoma beheading," Sept 27th 2014, CNN News.

http://www.cnn.com/2014/09/26/us/oklahom
a-beheading/

3. "Islamic Opening Prayer to Allah in the House of
    Representatives," Nov 14 2014, House Session
    Part 1, C-Span. http://www.c-
    span.org/video/?c4514851/islamic-opening-
    prayer-allah-house-representatives

4. Derek Harvey & Michael Pregent, "Who's to
    blame for Iraq crisis," Jun 12th 2014,
    http://www.cnn.com/2014/06/12/opinion/pre
    gent-harvey-northern-iraq-collapse/

5. Jonathan Broder, "Iraq's ISIS Fight Could Be a
    Second 'Awakening," Jan 27th 2014, Newsweek.
    http://www.newsweek.com/2015/02/06/awake
    ning-part-ii-301906.html

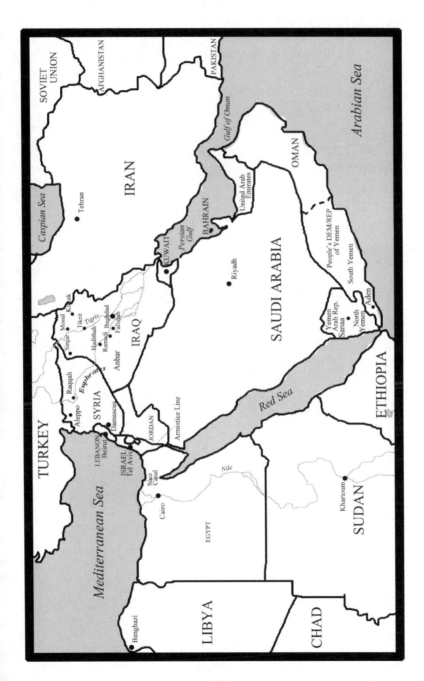

ABOUT THE AUTHOR

D.J. Ratkowski, a former United States Marine who spent time in the Middle East. Combat tested he received multiple awards while fighting in the Middle East, including a Presidential Citation. He attended school in Northern California and graduated with honors, Phi Theta Kappa, Beta Mu Zeta.

D.J. Ratkowski is also the author of
"Whiskey Sierra: The Devil Dog Chronicles"

You can follow his blog at www.djratkowski.com
@DJRatkowski